The Musical  *ol Child*

2-90

Helmut Moog

The Musical Experience of the Pre-school Child

Translated by Claudia Clarke

Schott Music

Acknowledgments

Grateful thanks are due to the following for permission to reproduce copyright material:

Ginn & Co. Ltd, 191 Spring Street, Lexington, Massachusetts, U.S.A. publishers of *Education for Musical Growth* by James L. Mursell

Prentice-Hall Inc., Englewood Cliffs, New Jersey, U.S.A. publishers of *Piaget and Knowledge* by Hans G. Furth

Hutchinson Publishing Group Ltd, 3 Fitzroy Square, London WIP 6JD publishers of *The Background to Music* by Harry Lowery

Aloys Henn Verlag KG, 5448 Kastellaun, Postfach, Germany publishers of *Beginn und erste Entwicklung des Musikerlebens im Kindesalter* by Helmut Moog

Original edition published in 1968 by B. Schott's Söhne, Mainz
English edition published in 1976 by Schott & Co. Ltd, 48 Great
Marlborough Street, London, WIV 2BN

ISBN 0 901938 06 8
Schott Edition No. 11154

Printed in Great Britain by
Heffers Printers Ltd, Cambridge

Contents

Translator's Preface

Art is some creation of man that appeals to his emotions and his intellect by means of his senses.
WILLIAM MORRIS

The present opposition between science and music can in large measure be traced to this disintegrating effect of the application of scientific method in music, yet no one can deny that the analytical method of science does lead to positive knowledge in the musical field. But it must be admitted that the musician also reaches positive results involving musical ideas, especially when at work as a composer balancing one musical idea against another and evolving new ideas from the presented material. His method is just the opposite of the scientist's and may well be described as intuitive. He deals in musical wholes and reaches his creative product in one bound rather than by carefully reasoned steps.
LOWERY *The Background to Music* 1952

These two quotations, which hint at the size and nature of the problem of applying scientific method to one of the arts, may suggest one reason why, in the extensive literature on child development, music has been so neglected, though in everyday life sounds of one kind or another play such an important part, the more so now that, thanks to modern technology, they can be so easily reproduced, magnified or distorted. Karel Pech, in his *Hearing in a Visual Age (Hören im optischen Zeitalter*. G. Braun, 1969), states that very small babies respond purposefully to sound before they can focus their eyes properly, yet, although more and more specialist studies of musical development have been published, a work on general development, such as Gesell's *The First Five Years*, still dismisses music most briefly. In the Soviet Union recent research has shown that the development of speech hearing and of musical hearing in young children does not follow a parallel course and that, as yet, the exact nature of the two systems of hearing has not been investigated (Zaporozhets and Elkonin, *Psychology of Pre-School Children*. English translation published by Massachusetts Institute of Technology, 1971.)
Das Musikerleben des Vorschulpflichtigen Kindes by H. Moog, was published

by Schott of Mainz in 1968. It is a summary of *Beginn und erste Entwicklung des Musikerlebens im Kindesalter* (Henn. Second edition 1967), a doctoral thesis for which the research was done by Dr Moog in 1960–1. Some material from the thesis is included in this edition, as the music used for the tests is printed in full in Chapter 2 of the 1967 edition of the thesis, and is given here in the Introduction, together with an English translation of the original German texts and a summary of the explanations of each test. In the introductory chapter to his book the author undertook the formidable task of explaining the ideas that lay behind his research with young children, and his reasons for planning his work as he did. All this need not concern practising teachers, for whom this work is primarily intended, and they would be well advised to begin with Chapter 2 and end with Chapter 1; if they find it necessary to tackle this chapter at all. It illustrates all too clearly the limitations of the written word in any language. In dealing with it I have been reminded continually of the differences between the English and the German academic traditions, and, for this reason, this part of the English version of the text and the sections of each chapter on general development are perhaps overburdened with footnotes. So I have tried to keep these to a minimum in the rest of the text. I have, of course, kept the author's references to his sources, simply adding a few more when the German terminology or thinking seems to differ widely from the English.

He has used a standard German manual of Child Psychology by Remplein. A comparable English work is Carmichael's *Manual of Child Psychology* (edited by Paul H. Mussen, Third edition 1970). The literature on this subject, in both English and German, is enormous and much of it reflects the school of psychology to which the particular author belongs. The summaries which Dr Moog gives at the beginning of each chapter are, therefore, only included in order to give a brief reminder of the context into which the research on musical development must be set. For English readers whose knowledge of psychology is limited, I add a short list of some of the books that I have found helpful during the work of translation.

K. Lovell, *An Introduction to Human Development*, Second edition 1969. Macmillan paperback.

Mary B. Sheridan, *The Developmental Progress of Infants and Young Children*. H.M.S.O. 1968.

N. Isaacs, *The Growth of Understanding in the Young Child*. A brief introduction to Piaget's work. Ward Lock, 1961.

R. Griffiths, *The Abilities of Babies*. University of London Press, 1954.

G. Revesz, *Introduction to the Psychology of Music*. Longmans, 1953. (A translation from the German edition of 1946, with revisions).

Three books have been invaluable:

A. T. Jersild, *Child Psychology*. Sixth edition 1968. Prentice-Hall.
This is much shorter than Carmichael and proved much more readable for the layman. It also stresses the effect which the assumptions of the observer have on the conclusions which he draws, and it gives a select bibliography, not an exhaustive one. Readers who wish to know the results of the most recent research must, of course, still refer to Carmichael's *Manual of Child Psychology*, 1970 edition.

Harry Lowery, *The Background to Music*. Hutchinson, 1952.
With its lucid explanations of the problems involved in applying scientific and philosophical method to one of the arts this book helped both towards an understanding of the ideas expressed in the German original and also with the means of expressing those ideas in relatively simple English.

H. G. Furth, *Piaget and Knowledge*. Prentice-Hall 1969.
This deals, among other things, with the relationship of psychology to other disciplines, and it has also helped with other problems, though I am only too aware, lacking any scientific training, of the limited extent to which I have been able to understand it. Why, in spite of the large expansion of music departments which has taken place in English universities during the past twenty years, is it still so difficult, except possibly within the context of the B.Ed., for a student to acquire at undergraduate level a basic knowledge of both the disciplines of music and of psychology? Fortunately for those who approach the question from a background of music an elementary textbook of psychology in relation to music is now available, since an English translation of the original Swedish text by E. Franklin has now appeared as *Music Education : Psychology and Method* (Harrap 1972). Maybe all the work going on in music for slow learners and handicapped children will gradually become known to teachers of normal children and to those responsible for training such teachers, and far more attention will be paid to the development of auditory perception and the faculty of hearing than has been given to this vitally important area of growth in many of the older books on child development.

Finally I should like to thank my sister, Miss Magda Clarke, who has helped me to check and revise the whole translation, and Dr Moog himself, who has checked my text against the German and clarified certain obscurities in the original.

CLAUDIA CLARKE
Southampton, April 1973

Introduction

The purpose of this book is to give some insight into the musical experience of the pre-school child. Parents and professional educators should be stimulated by it to think about how the musical environment of our youngest children should be planned. The book is addressed also to the psychologist, since musical experience can occupy an important position in the child's general experience. Some characteristics of general experience have recognizable parallels in musical experience, while on the other hand some peculiarities of musical experience explain some things in non-musical experience.

As psychological considerations have an appreciable effect on both the type of music making and the scope of musical training, nursery teachers especially will find opportunity to put the results of this investigation into practice. At the same time the development of musical experience from the earliest years should also be of interest to teachers of older children, since the reasons for difficulties in teaching music to older pupils are likely to be more apparent to a teacher who has some understanding of the stages of musical development in early childhood. Moreover, music courses should be planned so as to take into account the order in which children develop an awareness of the different elements of music in early childhood (Wilbert 1967; Abel-Struth 1967).

Since the genetic psychology of music may be regarded as the developmental phase of the psychology of music in general, some basic knowledge of the general psychology of music is indispensable for understanding the musical experience of early childhood. As this basic knowledge cannot be assumed, and as the results of research into musical experience are not widely known, the first chapter consists of a short discussion of some aspects of the general psychology of music which relate to questions of musical development in early childhood.

Introduction

The genetic psychology of music is a branch, not only of the general psychology of music, but also of developmental psychology in general. In the first case the study of it leads on to the study of mature musical experience; in the second case it is part of the psychology of the development of the whole individual. Therefore each of the chapters from 2 to 6, which are concerned with definite stages of musical development, will begin with a brief exposition of the corresponding stage of general development.

The results of several years of research are set out in the following pages. Over 8,000 individual tests were carried out with nearly 500 children and the observations of about 1,000 parents were evaluated. Whenever it was possible, an example of the subject's singing was recorded on tape, and many conclusions were drawn from a critical analysis of these songs. The broad empirical basis was necessary to give sufficient reliability to the findings in a field of psychology where comparatively little work has been done. Nevertheless the results of this work on the musical experience of the child, which are set out in the following chapters, often do little more than indicate problems that require further special research for their solution.

The experimental procedure that was followed was the method introduced into psychology by Marbe (1901) and developed later by the Würzburg school (K. Bühler 1907). In this method an experience is produced in the subject (W. Metzger 1966), either by setting a task (K. Bühler 1907) or by playing a few bars of music (W. Probst 1960). Immediately afterwards the subject reports on his experience to the researcher. This research procedure presupposes that the subject is able to observe his experience and report on it. So it cannot be applied in this form to children (K. Bühler 1930), for a child does not begin to make spoken comments on a stimulus until the age of two to three. Even then the child does not give a full account of his experience, as an adult does, but simply indicates *what* he has experienced. Yet even this is a great help, for, though the researcher has to rely entirely on observation in dealing with the very youngest children, from the third year onwards he can supplement his observations with reports from his young subjects and draw some conclusions about the relevant experience from what they tell him about that experience.

In its original form the activity of the researcher had to be limited to administering the tests and to recording the experiences reported to him.

In work with young children the observations of the researcher must, clearly, replace the reports of the subjects. There is a further difficulty, which makes work with children, as opposed to adults, even harder. It is this: with children few striking reactions can be observed. If during the playing of a musical test a child turns towards the source of stimulus one may assume that he experiences 'something'. That this 'something' is to do with music may only be indicated by an expression such as 'music', or just by '-sic', mostly with the accent on the first syllable;[1] by a forefinger pointing; or by the baby clearly turning towards the source of the sound and listening. The motor responses of the infants often tell us little more than that the experience has to do with music. In certain circumstances the facial expression may be interpreted, with caution, as rejection or acceptance. Thus the behaviour of small children gives only very general indications of what the experience produced by the experiment is, and the test procedure must be so arranged that a sufficiently detailed picture emerges from the slightest indications of the reactions of the young subjects. Each experiment must isolate an individual problem. If the experiments are arranged in this way and each has a specific purpose, then the very general indications given by the subjects can only refer to the specific matter being tested. They have the same effect as 'yes' or 'no' in answer to a decisive question (K. Bühler 1930). The accuracy of the result depends on the planning of the series of tests. Yet, because of the purpose of the investigation, there is a limit to the extent to which the researcher may try to isolate problems as he plans the series of tests. Genetic psychology is still so much in its early stages that we must get a general view of the musical experience of the child before investigations into individual questions can be undertaken.

The aim of this research is to investigate the stages of development. It is not simply a question of establishing the existence of specific types of musical experience in general, but of their place in child development. The best way to investigate the changes which take place during the development of musical experience is to take the development itself as the variable in the experiments and keep the experimental procedure constant. For this reason we played the same series of tests to all the young children tested, irrespective of their age group. The different responses could then be referred back to differences in stages of development, as well as to

1. In German, unlike English, the accent is on the second syllable.

individual differences (A. Busemann 1953). How far the question is one of genuinely different stages of development must then be ascertained by setting the results of the experiments in the context of the general development of the child. The series of tests played to the children was as follows.

Test Series 1. *Three Children's Songs*

1.1 *Ring-a-ring o'roses*

1. Rin-gel, Rangel, Ro – sen, schöne A – pri – ko – sen,

Veilchen und Vergissmeinnicht, alle kleinen Kin-der

setzen sich.

2. Ringel, Rangel, Reihe, sind der Kinder dreie,
   sitzen unterm Holderbusch, singen alle:
   'Husch, husch, husch!'

1. Ring-a-ring o' roses, fine apricots, violets and forget-me-nots, all the little children sit down.
2. Ring-a-ring o' roses, three children are sitting under an elder bush and all sing: 'Shh', Shh', Shh'.'

1.2 *The Gay Tyroleans*

1. Die Ti – ro – ler sind lustig, die Ti – ro – ler sind

froh, sie verkaufen ihr Bett-zeug und

schlafen auf Stroh. Ru – di – ru – di

ra – la – la   ra – la – la   ra – la – la

ru – di – ru – di   ra – la – la   ra – la – la – la

2. Die Tiroler sind lustig, di Tiroler sind froh,
   sie nehmen ein Weibchen und tanzen dazu.
3. Erst dreht sich das Weibchen, dann dreht sich der
   Mann, dann tanzen sie beide und fassen sich an.

1. The Tiroleans are merry, the Tiroleans are gay, they sell their bedding and sleep on straw. Rudirudi- etc.
2. The Tiroleans are merry, the Tiroleans are gay, they take a wife and dance with her. Rudirudi- etc.
3. The woman turns round first, then the man turns, then they waltz round together.

1.3 *Sleep, baby, sleep*

Schlaf, Kindlein, schlaf!   Der   Vater   hüt' die

Schaf.   Die   Mutter   schüttelt's   Bäumelein,   da

fällt herab   ein   Träumelein.   Schlaf, Kindlein schlaf!

1.3
1. Sleep, baby sleep,' Father watches the sheep. Mother shakes a little tree and then a little dream falls down. Sleep, baby sleep.

The purpose of this test was to present the simplest, the best known and the most suitable music for young children. Songs 1 and 3 were selected because parents and nursery teachers said they were the best known, and they occurred most frequently in books of children's songs. Song 2 was included, though it is much less well-known, because it is one of the few songs of this type which are in three-time. The songs were sung un-

5

accompanied, partly by a clear untrained girl's voice, and partly by three such voices in unison. This series was designed to provide answers to the following questions:

How does a child react to music which is generally considered to be most suitable for young children?

What is the relationship between the response to Test Series 1 and to the other series of tests?

Is any distinction made between the songs in two- and the songs in three-time?

To what extent and in what way do children sing during the performance or imitate it afterwards?

The third song was also to serve as a preparation for Series 4 and 5.

Test Series 2. *Three Combinations of Words and Rhythm*

2.1 *Words with rhythm*

This means a text with the words so arranged that they must be spoken rhythmically to make sense. The sense and the rhythmic pattern are of equal importance.

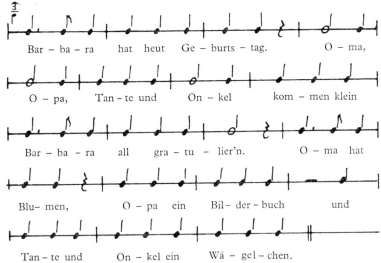

Barbara has a birthday today. Grandma, Grandad, Auntie and Uncle all come to congratulate Barbara. Grandma has flowers. Grandad a picture book and Auntie and Uncle a little swing.

2.2 *Rhythm with words added*

This occurs if words are spoken in a different rhythm from the one demanded by their sense. The rhythm is more important than the meaning of the words, which are deliberately not spoken in their natural rhythm.

When St. Nicholas comes, then the baby Christ will soon come too.

2.3 *Nonsense-word rhythm*

The distinguishing mark of a 'nonsense-word rhythm' is the absence of any meaning in the words. Sing-song syllables are strung together to make rhythmic patterns. For example many folk songs have such patterns as 'falala' or 'ding-dong' refrains, either in the middle of a verse or between the verses Words are used simply to provide a rhythmic pattern.

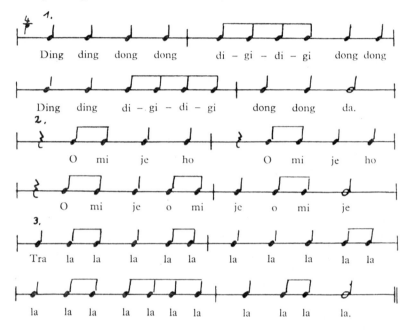

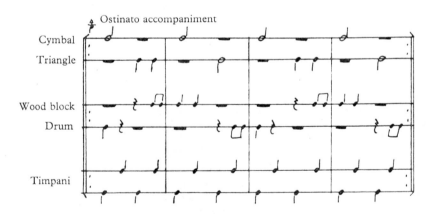

Ostinato accompaniment

These three tests were designed to provide examples of different relationships between music and speech. In the first the words are the most important and the rhythm follows their rhythm. In the second the rhythm comes first, and the words are fitted to it; the sense of the words is less important. In the third there is no attempt to convey meaning through the words, and the music is dominant, so the result is vocal music without sound of definite pitch. The last example was played twice, but only unpitched percussion instruments or clapping, stamping and finger snapping were used. The question to be answered was: would there be any musical response if the element of definite pitch was lacking? Would there be any difference in the response to the three tests?

Test Series 3. *'Pure' Rhythms*

3.1 *Rhythm for different percussion instruments*

Wood block
Tambourine
Cymbals

Carl Orff & Gunild Keetman, *Musik für Kinder*, vol. v, p. 91. Mainz n.d.

3.2 *Clapping-stamping rhythm*

Clapping
Knee-slapping
Stamping

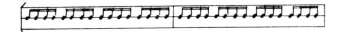

Orff & Keetman op. cit. p. 90

3.3 *Drum rhythm played on three hand-drums*

Introduction

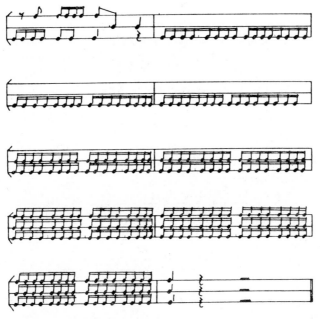

Orff & Keetman op. cit. p. 89

All three tests are taken from Vol. V of Orff-Schulwerk. The first was played on wood block, tambourine and cymbals, No. 2 was stamping, knee slapping and clapping, and No. 3 was played on three hand-drums. These 'pure rhythms' separate rhythm, both from words and from notes of fixed pitch. But differences of pitch are not completely absent since different fields of sound associated with different instrumental colours are used, as are different mixtures of sound. The first test has a very rich sound, but the volume was kept down so that the children would not be frightened. The total effect of the sound is more obvious than the rhythmic pattern; yet, though this effect is achieved through the combination of the rhythm and the instrumentation, the overall effect is of a torrent of sound. The clapping-stamping rhythm in the second test is in the sharpest contrast to the full sonority of the first. Only one sound is heard at a time and there is not much difference between the kinds of sounds used. So the rhythmic pattern is more apparent than in the first test. In the third test three similar instruments were used; so there is little mixing of quality, though the test starts with a single drum, continues with two drums playing the same rhythm and then three drums all playing different rhythms, before it ends in a unison passage. Rhythmic sounds produce responses at more than one level and the sense impression produced by the sound as a whole is distinct from the purely rhythmic element. The latter may consist of one or more voices. If different rhythms are played the effect is then one of polyphony; if the same rhythm is played by more than one instrument then the effect is a mixing of instrumental colour.

Test Series 4. *Instrumental Music*

4.1 *Twelve-note melody*

4.1 From Helmut Moog, *Bread from Stones*. A musical play for children, with solo voices, choir and orchestra. Unpublished. 1957

4.2 *Extract from the first movement of the Fourth Symphony by Anton*
Bruckner

From Eulenburg Score (Bruckner Symphony No. 4)
pages 2–7 inclusive

4.3 *Pop song, 'Seeman, lass das Traümen'*

See – mann, lass das Träu–men, denk nicht

an Zu – haus ! See – mann, Wind und

Wel – len ru – fen dich hin – aus:

Dei–ne Heimat ist das Meer, dei–ne Freunde sind die

Ster–ne ü–ber Ri – o und Schanghai,

ü–ber Ba–li und Ha – waii. Deine Lie–be ist dein

Schiff, deine ·Sehnsucht ist die Fer – ne

und nur ih–nen bist du treu ein Le – ben

lang

4.4 *String quartet, 'Sleep, baby, sleep'*

The twelve-note melody is from a work for children, written by the author in 1957, *Bread from Stones*. The melody was played on a recorder and is unmeasured, like plainsong, so that both rhythm and instrumental colour were reduced to a minimum. The element of pitch predominates. Dodecaphony was chosen rather than the conventional major or minor tonality to avoid the possibility of the melody awakening any harmonic response. This test was included to try to determine how children hear differences of pitch. The extract from Bruckner's *Fourth Symphony* (bars 27–75), after seven bars which are rhythmically as neutral as test 4.1, builds up into an overpowering mountain of sound, with much repetition of short rhythmic figures. So, in rhythm and tone colour, it is in the sharpest contrast to 4.1. However, it is the harmony, even more than the rhythm and tone colour, which is the important element in this symphony. The pop song, 'Sailor', was taken from the record Polydor No. 24177; the arrangement was not made available for research purposes. According to the publisher, Gerig of Cologne, it was one of the most widely-sold hit songs of 1960. Of all types of music, this is the most widely listened to today. Music educators seem more united in their stand against pop music than on any other matter, but the fact that it is not taught in school is no reason for not including it in this series of tests. Strictly speaking it should not be included in Test Series 4 since it is accompanied vocal music, but the instrumental accompaniment makes it quite different from the songs in the first series of tests. Also it forms a complete contrast with the extract from the symphony and with the 'tame' piece for quartet. It is included to find out how a child reacts to a pop song. 'Sleep, baby, sleep' is arranged for string quartet in the simplest possible way, with no passing notes.

Questions to be answered by this test series were: At what age do children begin to be able to recognize a song they know when it is played on an instrument? Are they capable of appreciating harmony? This series also prepares for series 5, since the same melody is used for the cacophonies.

Test Series 5. *Cacophonies*

1. *String quartet piece from Series 4.4 with altered viola part*

2. *String quartet piece from Series 4.4 with altered second violin, viola and cello parts*

3. *Homorhythmic cacophony (Four melodies played simultaneously so that the keys of B major, B flat major, C major and D major are heard at the same time)*

In this series of tests the validity of Wicke's observation that children are not disturbed by a displacement of a semitone or a whole tone is systematically investigated. The lullaby, 'Sleep, baby, sleep' was already known by many of the subjects before they were tested, and those who did not know it already heard it several times in series 1 and series 4. In 5.2 the viola part is raised a semitone and no great musical gift was required for the effect to be felt as disturbing, especially as it came immediately after 4.4. Test 5.2 is exactly the same as that which Wicke used: second violin, viola and cello are a semitone higher than the first violin. This sounds horrid, even to a moderately musical adult. Test 5.3 consists of four different melodies in four different keys, B flat, B, C and D major, played simultaneously, so that major and minor seconds are sounded together the whole time. It is hard to imagine a more unpleasant collection of dissonances. All three tests are written in a note-against-note style, and each part on its own would sound pleasant; so that any sign of displeasure can only be interpreted as arising from the cacophony. Anyone with any capacity for hearing harmony would show some sign of displeasure. What would our young subject do?

Test Series 6. *Nonmusical Noises*

1. *Sound of a vacuum cleaner*
2. *Traffic noise*

The sound of the vacuum cleaner was heard for about twenty seconds; it consisted of the motor starting, the vacuum cleaner working and being switched off. Similarly the noise of traffic at a busy crossroads was heard for about twenty seconds; the sound of a car starting is clearly recognisable, also the sound of changing gears. In order to set some limit to musical response, we decided to finish the series of tests with nonmusical sounds.

The tests were played to children aged six months, nine months, a year, eighteen months, two years, two and a half, three years, three and a half, four and a half, and five and a half. The difference in age between each group of subjects was thus sufficiently large to show different stages of development, and yet small enough to see the whole in perspective. The statements about musical experience in the first few months of life are based entirely on a series of observations, since the conditions necessary for systematic experiments did not exist. A more detailed account of part of the investigation was published under the title *Beginn und erste Entwicklung des Musikerlebens beim Kinde* (Thesis. Cologne 1963; 2nd edition, Ratingen 1967) and this appears here in a shortened form.

We should like to thank, most warmly, all parents, nursery teachers and nurses who have helped to make this investigation possible. A special word of thanks is due to my honoured teacher, Professor Dr Maria Krudewig, who assisted with the research until the last days of her life.

1 · Basic Questions of the General Psychology of Music

1. Music and Musical Experience

Musical experience has something to do with music; it is this which distinguishes it from other kinds of experience. The apparently obvious statement, which most people would accept as true, does not express adequately the nature of the relationship between musical experience and music, that is, how far the nature of music itself determines the nature of musical experience. Anyone who stops to ask the question, 'What is music?' is immediately faced with the difficult problem of finding a verbal definition, though, of course, everyone knows what is meant by the word. Two standard German dictionaries (J. and W. Grimm 1885, vol. 6, and F. Kluge 1957) gives as a synonym for 'music' the word '*Tonkunst*'.[1] Neither the Greek conception '*mousike*' (T. Georgiades 1954) nor the mediaeval term '*musica*' (H. Hüschen, typescript, 1955) can be equated with 'the art of sound' [i.e. *Tonkunst* in German]. Objections have also been raised by Kurt Sachs against identifying the German word '*Musik*' with 'the art of sound' in so far as not all music can claim for itself the title of nobility implied by the word art. However he, like everyone else, never questions the assumption that music always has something to do with tones or sounds. (K. Sachs 1921).[2]

1. *Tonkunst* means literally 'the art of sound'.

2. The definition given in the Oxford English Dictionary would start off a different process of verbal reasoning. It runs: '(1) that one of the fine arts concerned with the combination of sounds with a view to beauty of form and expression of emotion: also the science of the laws or principles (of melody, harmony, rhythm) by which this art is regulated; (2) sounds in melodic or harmonic combination, whether produced by voices or instruments'.

Detailed investigations of the relationship between music and sound have led to the conclusion that 'the perception of sounds is the only absolutely essential factor in musical experience' (W. Probst 1960, p. 53; also R. Descartes 1650; G. Albersheim 1939).[1] Perceived sounds may also be replaced by imagined ones. In other words, without perceived or imagined sounds there can be no music.

This reference to sounds, which determines the existence or non-existence of music, compels us to ask a further question: 'What is a sound?' E. Kurth helps with a verbal definition at the beginning of his *Psychology of Music*. He writes: 'What we call a sound does not have any mode of existence outside human experience; only the thing which causes it belongs to the external world'. (E. Kurth, Bern 1947, p. 1.)[2]

Until they are heard, sounds only exist as vibrations. Vibrations arise when material is set in motion, but if they are too fast or too slow we cannot hear them. We can see the effect of vibrations of very high frequency but we are unable to hear the slightest thing, and exactly the same thing happens with vibrations below the audible frequency range. In both cases there are vibrations but no sounds. *A sound can only be produced by the interaction of the vibrations and the person who hears them*. Here the word 'hears' must be understood in an analogous sense to the word 'paints' in the sentence: Someone paints the picture.

It is hearing only, the action of the person who has the experience, that creates the sound (G. Revesz 1946; A. D. Cherbuliez 1941). The vibrations that cause the sound are simply the necessary external source of stimulus for this action. A gramophone does not produce music; it produces vibrations in the air. If these frequencies are not heard, then there is no music. The personality and environment of the hearer determine the nature of the music heard. He creates the music by hearing it, and, con-

1. The last reference is quoted in full in Moog, *Beginn und Erste Entwicklung des Musikerlebens im Kindesalter* 1967, p. 39. 'If there is insufficient ability to distinguish differences of pitch [*Tonhoehenauffassung*] all the approaches to the art of sound are blocked'. For a full discussion in English of this question see G. Revesz, *Psychology of Music*, 1953, chapter LV.

2. '*Nirgends in der Welt schweift jene eigentümliche Wesenheit umher die uns als Ton vertraut ist; nur was ihn verursacht gehört der Aussenwelt an*'. I have paraphrased the first sentence of Kurth, *Psychology of Music*, which for a German author is a well-known quotation. The book has not been translated into English.

sequently, music has no independent existence outside the person who experiences it.[1]

How does it come about that music can be regarded, in non-scientific and non-psychological circles, as something outside the self?

The reason for this lies in the peculiar way in which we experience music. We experience music – even though we ourselves create it – by projecting it outside ourselves into the place where its source of stimulus arises. For example, when we hear the sound of a trumpet we detach this sound from the complex of impressions in our ear, and attach it to the instrument which produced the stimulus. In a similar way eidetic (spontaneous) musical experience, or even creative musical experience that did not arise from an external source, is projected outwards and is made objective in the truest sense of the word. The composer who has to have in mind sound images of his music as he writes it down, does not have these 'in himself' but hears them coming from outside.

Till now, two terms have been used for the vibrations which cause musical experience. These are corresponding stimulus, and source of stimulus. The latter expression is nearer to the true facts, as musical experience is an interaction between the stimulus and the hearer, and the two do not always agree exactly. Rhythmic errors are, up to a point, corrected by the listener. Unrhythmical stimuli – e.g. a dripping tap – are heard in a rhythmical form. Rests may be supplied to complete a small musical form (Moog 1967). A choir, practising a voice training exercise of three bars of 4/4 time, as it repeats the exercise instinctively supplies a bar of silence between repetitions, to make a four bar phrase, without being asked to do so.

Research by Stephanie has shown that we equate differences of pitch up to a quarter tone (H. Stephanie 1956). When voices cross in linear counterpoint we hear the note in which the voices cross as tending in two

1. Harry Lowery, *The Background to Music*, 1952, p. 18, explains this as follows: 'Music is not to be identified with the production of vibrations, the transmission through the air of waves due to vibratory disturbances and the resulting motions of the mechanism of the ear. All these are purely physical or objective matters and do not even constitute *sounds*, still less music. Not until some link has been established between the chain of physical events and the hearer's mind, is it correct to say that sounds have been heard, and not until the hearer's mind has done work upon the sounds, can it be said that they are melodious or harmonious or rhythmical, possessing musical value'.

directions, even when the source of stimulus is on the keyboard and is only sounded once. Melodies may be heard as standing out from accompanying figures.[1]

This list of considerable differences between the music that is actually heard and the relevant source of stimulus shows how important a part the subjective activity of hearing plays in the creation of musical experience (J. F. Herbart 1831). There must be some source of stimulus, real or imagined, for musical experience to take place, but we have already shown that it is the experience of hearing which creates music from the source of stimulus, and this experience may to a certain extent also modify or complete the stimulus signal. This conclusion, that the vibrations which produce music only become music when they are heard, does not contradict the proposition stated at the beginning, that the experience can only be a musical one, since it is caused by music and not by anything else. The interaction between the hearing and the vibrations is the essential condition, whichever way we look at the process.

Up till now the discussion has been of musical experience as a whole. This would seem to be the best starting point; for in a full musical experience (W. Probst 1960) the human consciousness is so totally involved that all sense of time and space may be lost. But even if such an intense experience is comparatively rare, a considerable part of the personality is always involved.

Musical experience is not merely hearing or merely thinking, nor is it mere feeling, though this last is the opinion one most frequently meets with. It forms a totality, in which other fundamental forms of experience as well as those already mentioned play their part.

Not only in psychology, but also in education, medicine and natural science some researchers have adopted a holistic point of view, and have tried to consider the organism as a whole.

Anyone who sets out to research into experience as an organic whole should try to gain detailed knowledge of the inner workings of the personality in its entirety. He will no more be able to dispense with studies of parts of the scientific field than a doctor can dispense with studies of parts

---

1. S. Nelson, *The Violin and Viola*, 1972, p. 251, gives many further examples related to problems of orchestral tuning and adds 'A soloist who feels his tone drowned by the orchestra may sing or play a little sharper than the general pitch, consciously or unconsciously, to make himself heard: only if he over-exaggerates this effect will the audience notice'.

of the anatomy in seeking to understand the organism as a whole. So the next sections of this chapter will deal separately with some of the special fields of musical experience, in order to arrive at a better understanding of the experience as a whole by concentrating on one aspect of it at a time.[1]

2. Sensory Perception in Musical Experience

As far as the senses are concerned music, obviously, is to do with hearing; and the perception of it, being auditory, differs from visual and other forms of perception (Krudewig 1953). Since it is a series of perceptible events in time, it is tied to time in a way in which perceptions of sight and touch are not. Acoustical phenomena never exist in a single point of time. The only thing in a melody which exists as a source of stimulus in the 'absolute present', the 'point of change' between the past and the future, is a pinpoint fraction of a vibration. In other words: in the absolute present the air between two people talking to each other only vibrates in the shortest imaginable interval, too small for any sound – let alone a word – to be caught; also, sounds only exist as a series and not simultaneously in every 'point of time' (F. Brentano 1920, p. 6f). The ebb and flow of anything which is heard, whether it is noise, speech or music, must of necessity be felt to be within the passage of time.[2] The mind must be capable of an awareness of the passage of time over a longer span than the 'immediate now', before a structure which takes place within time can be perceived as a succession of events. This ability has been referred to as 'the mental present' (M. Krudewig 1961–62; A. Welleck 1963).[3] It includes part of the immediate experience of the past and looks forward

1. See also H. G. Furth, *Piaget and Knowledge*, 1969, p. 202, on the need for collaboration between scientists and philosophers in the study of the ways in which we acquire knowledge.

2. Jean Piaget, *The Child's Conception of Time*. English edition 1969, p. 268. 'We cannot see or perceive time as such since, unlike space or velocity it does not impinge upon our senses. All we can perceive is events i.e. motions, actions, speeds and their results. Thus temporal successions are determined by the order of events, and durations either by their motions, i.e. by distances covered at given velocities, or else by actions, i.e. the work done at a given rate'.

3. This philosophical abstraction 'mental present' (*seelische Gegenwart*) is a concept, English readers may well find difficult to grasp. Piaget's book, which was published in French in 1927, but not in an English translation until 1969, gives a full account of his research into this difficult subject, and of its many different ramifications.

also towards the future, and proceeds – like everything else which exists – in a continuum which is independent of experience and as regular as a clock. It only exists in the ever present 'now' between the absolute past and the absolute future, but the action of experience joins the immediate past to this 'now' and relates it to the future, selecting and modifying the content of the present moment as that moves into the future.

Thus noise, speech and music, the three things concerned with hearing, are equally tied to the mental present. What distinguishes one from another? What is the distinction between music and noise? One obvious difference is in the relationship of noise and music to things. Noises give us audible information about things. The rattling of an old car, the noise of a motor, the creaking of a door, tell us something about our environment. If we cannot relate the noise to a thing, we often observe a tendency in ourselves to discover what was making the noise by looking around us. Acoustical data on their own do not give us enough information about the surrounding world. Often they only provide us with the urge to orientate ourselves visually to our surroundings. There are only a few noises which we can distinguish accurately by the sound alone: we can only do so with sounds such as the footsteps of a near relative, or noises in our own home, etc.

Four musicians who were sitting by a wide open window on a hot summer evening and heard the sound of a moped and then noises which indicated an accident, were not accepted by a court of law as witnesses to drunken driving when the driver maintained he was only pushing the machine. The witnesses excused their uncertainty by saying that they had *only heard* the accident. 'There is a perfect and comprehensive world of objects . . . only in the field of sight' (M. Krudewig 1953, p. 96). Noises certainly need to be related to objects, but they give us such inexact information about objects that the perception needs to be completed by the addition of the visual impression.[1] What about the relationship between speech and the world of objects? 'When speech is considered in relation to objects, at first sight the sound quality appears to predominate' (M. Krudewig 1953, p. 96). On looking more closely at it, one comes to the conclusion that it is not speech itself, but the meaning of speech, which is concerned with the world of objects. Take for example the word 'cup-

---

1. H. G. Furth, *Piaget and Knowledge*, 1969, p. 136, 'Notions of time and space are intimately related'.

board'. The thing is not the word 'cupboard', but the piece of furniture to which the word refers. 'The objective part of language is not the sound quality but the *substance* of what is said, for which it acts as a symbol' (H. Moog 1967, p. 79).

What is the relationship of music to the world of objective reality? Music is not the noise of an object, neither is it a symbol in sound for an object – as is language – in which thought and images of objects are directly attached to the symbol. The musical sound does not give information *about* anything, nor does it stand as a representative *for* anything. It is neither source of information nor symbol. Music does indeed use sensory material, but there is much more to it than there is to hearing because 'in music the main concern is with the working-up of the material presented to the mind through the ear into a meaningful assemblage of sounds'.[1] When it becomes music, hearing acquires an aesthetic quality just because it is not like some railway junction on the line to objects. As a medium of communication it does not function in the same way as language and does not 'travel towards reality' (N. Hartmann 1953, p. 52). Thus sound may be invested with aesthetic value, and evoke pleasure. The whole sensory process of perceiving music may produce pleasure. If one thinks of the variety of timbre of flutes, trumpets, strings and other instruments, and reminds oneself of the different effects which may be created by altering the instrumentation one will beware of underestimating this purely sensory element in music. However, if music is to be considered as something more than mere sound quality we must take into account more than the purely sensory element. If melodies, harmonies and musical forms are to be experienced, cognitive abilities also are needed.[2]

3. Musical Thinking

Everyone would agree that music is a matter of feeling and mood. But it is by no means usual today to connect music with thinking, though many references have been made in the literature on music education to the

1. Harry Lowery, *Background to Music*, 1952, p. 37.

2. Buck (1935), quoted by Lowery, *ibid.*, p. 22, 'Music is an activity of the mind. I find that almost everybody, especially musicians, denies that, and even hotly resents it'.

music of antiquity and to mediaeval music (Haase 1950; G. Götsch 1953; Scheidler 1953) which could have been used today to stress the importance of the cognitive element. The position of music in the quadrivium and the conception of music in both classical antiquity and in mediaeval times, when compared with much of our own musical terminology (H. Hüschen 1955), show clearly that the relationship between music and thinking is a problem worthy of our consideration.

So it is all the more surprising to find Haase maintaining that there is no connection between the two, when he firmly states that 'education in the arts' ['*musische Erziehung*', in German] can neither sharpen the intelligence nor strengthen the will (Haase 1950, p. 40). For Scheidler musical activity is 'a natural expression of one's feelings and inclination' (Scheidler 1952, p. 11). Kestenberg too (1921) emphasizes the importance of feeling in artistic activity though he does not go so far as to exclude all mental activity from music.

A large number of authorities, among them Herbart (1831), Hanslick (1854), Hegel (1939), Schering (1941), Kurth (1947), Adorno (1958), agree that thinking plays a considerable part in musical experience and, in contrast to the writers mentioned in the last sentence, they support their opinions with reasoned arguments. However, it is not enough simply to state that musical experience involves thinking. It is even more important to try to determine what some of the chief characteristics of this sort of thinking are.[1] So we will begin by attempting a general definition of thinking.

Relations and their structure can only be arrived at through thinking, so thinking may most briefly be defined as the grasping of relations (Krudewig 1947). This can take place according to Krudewig (1947) either in thinking behaviour, that is, over a longer period of time, or in a short single instant. K. Bühler distinguishes three types of thinking: first, consciousness of relation; second, consciousness of rules; and third, purely formal intelligence (Bühler 1907).[2] But he notes too that the two last named types of thinking include some consciousness of relation. Knowledge and the application of rules are of necessity concerned with

1. Combarieu, quoted by Lowery, *Background to Music*, 1952, p. 18, '*La musique est l'art de penser avec les sons*'.

2. The translation of this passage is taken from Jean Piaget, *Growth of Intelligence*, p. 23, where a clear summary of Bühler's theories is given.

relations, in that they are the hypothetical or actual application of general principles to specific circumstances, even though a strong memory element is undeniably present; it is no doubt this which led Bühler to draw a distinction between 'consciousness of rules' and 'consciousness of relations'. The same applies to things known, things intended, things seen as object or category, which Bühler designates 'intentions'. The thing known comes out of the store of knowledge in the memory. But its emergence is not a matter of chance, it comes rather as a thought about a specific matter, or group of events. This relatedness is the essential characteristic of Bühler's 'intentions', and it too is included in the definition of thinking as 'consciousness of relation'.

Bühler was able to demonstrate the difference between thinking and sensory perception experimentally when he proved that thinking was still going on without the subject matter of the thinking necessarily being present to the senses. This highly important proof does not contradict the fact that we do not only think with concepts which have no sensory associations, but we far more often use ideas which have their roots in some sense impression. In fact, thinking is normally based on sensory data (Bühler 1907), that is, the relations which are recognized rest on perceived or imagined subject matter or on sensory symbols of concepts which are not in themselves of a sensory nature.[1]

Thinking which does not in some way rest on sensory impressions could then only be possible as a momentary flash of insight, and this would bring with it the tendency to look for supporting evidence from the senses.

The distinction between abstract and concrete thinking is determined more by the subject matter than by different processes of thought. In the one the given concepts are abstract, in the other these are concrete. Thus it is the nature of the subject matter which determines the nature of the thinking. Musical thinking works with concepts which are perceived or imagined sounds. A sound remains isolated on its own unless it is recognized as having a meaningful relation to the sounds which come before

1. See H. G. Furth, *Piaget and Knowledge*, 1969, p. 66ff for a summary of different philosophical theories of knowledge and the difficulties which have arisen through confusion in the use of language. The summary which Moog gives here of Bühler's theories, clearly shows the philosophical tradition in which he was brought up, and which helps to account for many of the difficulties he has experienced in trying to express in words many of his ideas about music.

and after it, and if the two sounds occur simultaneously a relationship between them must be grasped. Sensory perception on its own cannot do this: the mind has to operate on the sense impression which the ears receive.

Something spoken may well provide the hearer with food for thought long after the sounds of speech have died away. In the fields of measurement and number too, as in many other fields, the sensory impression is a medium of communication that is not absolutely necessary so long as the process of communication is clear. Once the meaning is grasped, then further relations may be set up as thinking goes on. The meaning is grasped by the mind: the senses only serve as a means of transmission and a support. So there are two factors in musical experience: the mental and the sensory; and the concepts for musical thinking are sound perceived by the senses. The senses register the pitch, duration, intensity and timbre of the individual sounds, while the mind relates each element in the single sounds – pitch, duration, etc. – to the same element in the rest of the sounds in the series, since it is the relationship between the different sounds in the series which provides the material for the whole process of musical thought. But since – as has already been established – music is a self-contained art, whose meaning is conveyed through the senses, the sensory basis can never be lacking in musical thinking.[1] *Musical thinking, therefore, consists in establishing relationships between concepts which are perceived by the sense of hearing.*

The sound perceived by the sense of hearing need not necessarily be connected with an object. The musical sound may be recognised by the senses as flute-, violin- or trumpet-tone, that is, its timbre may be identified mentally with one which has been previously experienced. But that is not, musically speaking, the real significance of the sound: it is merely the auditory aspect of it. The actual musical essence of the sound lies precisely in this *sensory* quality.

The sensory nature of its concepts distinguishes musical thinking not only from thinking which is related to objects but also from other types of thinking. For example, mathematical thinking is also pure thought not related to objects. But there is this difference between musical and mathematical thinking: the first deals with concepts perceived by the sense of

---

1. cf. Harry Lowery, *The Background to Music*, 1952, p. 21, 'The materials of music are themselves mental phenomena'.

hearing; the second works with abstractions. If symbols which may be perceived by the senses are introduced into mathematics they do not relate to something concrete: in mathematical thinking symbols represent abstract concepts, for mathematical thinking is unrelated to objects. Musical thinking however, though unrelated to objects, is not in the least abstract. Its concepts are sounds which are heard and which are always present in a concrete form. Concrete thinking uses concepts which are either present in a *concrete* form, or are single events which may have been recalled by the memory. This definition applies also to musical thinking. The concept must be a sound heard, or a sound which has been heard at some time or other.

In the field of seeing, the sensory element must always have some sort of connection with an object, however slight that connection may be. *It is only in music that thinking rests on sensory concepts which are unrelated to objects. Only in music do we have something which is sensory and concrete without any relationship to objects.*

Musical thinking has this in common with thinking related to objects: it deals with relationships which arise through sensory impressions. It differs from thinking related to objects in that the subject matter of music does not refer back to things but possesses a value of its own: it has one characteristic in common with mathematical thinking: both have no direct relationship to objects; but it is distinguished from mathematical thinking by the concrete nature of its sensory concepts. The fact that musical thinking rests on sensory impressions means that it may present fewer intellectual difficulties than mathematical thinking, but the fact must also be faced that, in its highest form, musical thinking presents an additional difficulty in that it demands sensory activity at the same time as intellectual activity.

Musical experience at its most elementary level always has a broad sensory basis. Thus music which makes few intellectual demands is always rich in sound. Simple music is often simple because it has taken on something which helps to make it simple: that is, some relationship to objects – as happens in programme music, where the sound indicates something besides the sense of the music purely as music. Words may also be used as a simplifying factor, since it is always easier to think in terms of objects than without them.

The element of music connected with time, which is so difficult to grasp intellectually, is experienced at the most elementary level simply as physical rhythm. Then the intellect may learn to grasp this time element, if the body helps by making objective, concrete, physical movements. In simple music, rhythm provides a strong formative element, not by great variety of rhythm, but rather through short rhythmic figures persistently repeated. Repetitions of dance rhythms are much less difficult to grasp mentally than musical forms that extend over a longer period of time, because it is difficult for the hearer to perceive these forms as a whole; the same applies to forms in which the rhythm is perpetually changing.

4. Music and Language

Music and language are man made and are peculiar to man and his fellow men. In vocal music there is a close inner connection between music and language. The text not only contributes its content and meaning to the total effect – so that music which would otherwise be non-objective is related in some way to an object; it also enriches the sound with a kind of additional instrument.

The extent to which the sound of the words enriches the total sound may be measured by imagining a recitative with the vocal line replaced by an instrument. Then, instead of the variety of sound in the words, only *one* instrumental colour could be heard. The objection that it is not the missing *sound* of the words which makes the experience poorer, but the missing *meaning*, is not valid. One can substitute, for purposes of comparison, a recitative in a foreign language. Foreign vocal works, indeed whole operas, may be performed in a foreign language in order to keep the original sound.

The part which carries the meaning is comparatively small in the total effect of the sound of language. In European languages it is chiefly the form of the speech sound which conveys the objective meaning. Rhythmic variations only play a small part in modifying the meaning. For example the words 'live' and 'leave' are only distinguished by the different length of the sound. Differences of pitch are not used at all to communicate objective meaning. Whether one speaks in a higher or lower tone of voice, within a wider or narrower melodic range, the sense of the words does not alter.

Speakers of European languages may use variations in tempo and emphasis, as well as differences of pitch, to give additional, subjective meaning to what they say. The extent to which rhythmic and pitch differences communicate the temperament and the mood of the speaker would be a subject of study on its own.

In Asian languages the situation is quite different. In Japanese, rhythmic differences alter the meaning slightly, much more than in German. Chinese uses different 'speech tones' to distinguish between different meanings of words. In classical Chinese there are four, and in Chinese dialects as many as seven different 'speech tones'. For our purposes it is important that a spoken language be considered as a total complex, to understand which the hearer only has to abstract and consider the phonetic sound of the words, and something of their rhythmic pattern. These linguistic conventions must be accepted by both speaker and listener if intelligible communication is to take place. Meaning cannot be conveyed through language unless the laws of that particular language are observed.

The total sound of speech – not only that part of it which conveys meaning – is, since it is a sound, subject to the laws of aesthetics. It is 'music in language'. In vocal music this total sound is given a definite musical function; it has aesthetic quality because it is sound; it has a rhythmic form and, though it does not have a fixed pitch, it still lies within a given frequency range. The sound of the words is on an equal footing with rhythm, pitch and harmony, as a formative element in music. In German and other European languages pitch differences do not serve to convey meaning and, therefore, broad sweeping melodies, or even melodies with wide leaps, have hardly any adverse effect on the intelligibility of the words so long as the speech rhythm is more or less preserved. In song, sounds of fixed pitch are used, and thus a musical pitch-pattern is superimposed on the natural sound-pattern of spoken words. This pattern is inherent in speech, even in those languages which do not use pitch differences to convey meaning.

Things are not quite so simple when it comes to the relationship between rhythmic pattern and language. Rhythmic patterns, unlike variations of pitch, are not independent of the sense of the words. That is why the linguistic conventions may easily come into conflict with aesthetic principles when language and rhythm are considered together. Kierkegaard (1939) has dealt with the role of musical elements – timbre and rhythm – in the spoken word. According to him, there is always some musical element present in language, even in prose – 'the language form that is furthest removed from music'. The musical element in speech 'manifests itself more and more strongly at different levels in the poetic form . . . until at last the musical has been developed so strongly that language ceases and everything becomes music.'[1]

Music is tied to sound, but not necessarily to sounds which can be accommodated diatonically. If the concept 'music' were to be considered in such a narrow sense, then a large part of primitive music, folk dances and songs, percussion solos in modern dance music, and children's songs of indeterminate pitch would be excluded. Orff's rhythmic accompaniments to speech, and indeed every sound produced by rhythm instruments, would then not be classified as music or as a source of musical sound. *We are therefore justified in speaking of music even where fixed pitch is lacking, since rhythmic pattern and spoken language are experienced in the same way as music, and not as noise, nor like language considered as a whole.* Even though it is not incorporated into a tonal system the rhythmic sound of speech has musical power.

The different relationship between rhythm and speech may be classified under three headings.

a. *Words with Rhythm*

This group consists of words and phrases so arranged that they can only be spoken meaningfully when they are given a rhythmic form. The sense of the words must be preserved. Rhythmic pattern and the conveying of meaning are equally important.

b. *Rhythms with Added Words*

The opposite of the combination of words and rhythm mentioned above is shown by the 'rhythms with words added'. These occur when words are added to an existing rhythm whose rhythmic pattern differs from that of the words. The sense of the words is distorted. The rhythmic pattern is of primary importance; the sense of the words is secondary and is pushed into the background. Messerschmid has shown that the same distinction in combinations of words and rhythms as we have noted under a and b,

1. See Kierkegaard, *Either/Or*, Vol.1 p.55, translated by D. F. and L. M. Swenson, O.U.P. 1944, for the full English text of the passage summarized here.

exists in the old hymns, though he has not given it a label (F. Messerschmid 1929–30).

c. *Nonsense-word Rhythms*

In this group the rhythmic element predominates even more. At the same time the characteristic rhythm of the words is given greater importance. The communicative function of speech is completely abandoned. Nonsense words and syllables are strung together according to the demands of the rhythmic pattern. The effect of the rhythmic pattern of sound is the only thing that determines the choice of words and syllables. Speech becomes, so to speak, a rhythm instrument. The three forms mentioned above are met with, in practice, chiefly as mixed forms. A song whose first verse takes on the rhythm appropriate to the words must, if possible, fit to the same rhythm the words of the verses following; so that a combination of words and rhythm in the sense of our second group ensues. A refrain to each verse, such as 'Fa-la-la' or 'Ding-dong', would be considered as a nonsense-word rhythm and be placed in our last group. The role of music increases from the first to the third group, while that of speech diminishes. The borderland between music and language is of special importance in work in genetic psychology because the earliest musical experiences of children take place to a large extent in this realm. Here observers have noted differences of language experience and musical experience, as well as areas where the two overlap.

5. Feeling in Musical Experience

In everyday speech the word 'feeling' is used for four totally different concepts. For example a material may 'feel' rough, soft, or hard. In this case 'feel' corresponds to 'touch'. Something else is meant when someone says he does not 'feel' well. Here it is 'the physical sensation of his own body' (J. Volkelt 1937) that is called 'feeling'. A further difference is indicated if a matter is recognised or judged to be 'purely a matter of feeling'. Then the word 'feeling' is applied to unclear, unanalysed, vague thoughts and images (H. Volkelt 1937). The feeling experienced by someone who has just fallen in love or just passed an examination differs yet again from the three first named feelings.

In scientific usage the word 'feeling' is not used in the sense of 'touch'. But this use of the word 'feeling' in everyday speech points clearly to a connection between the emotional and the physical.

Feeling as 'something within the physical state' applies psychologically too, in that the physical state of a person plays a significant part in determining his overall mood (H. Volkelt 1937). Lindworsky (1928) went so far as to call sensations of the organs of the body the characteristic experiences of feeling; James (1884) and Lange (1887) identified these with feelings, thus surely overestimating their importance.

It is wrong to use the term 'feeling' in the sense of 'a particular experience or perception' if the term 'feeling' does not imply some emotional experience in perception. In other words: perception and comprehension are inextricably bound up with it. Feeling is neither the result of a perceptual content nor the action of the perception itself. Feeling is essentially different from sensation, perception and thinking, precisely in this respect: it is not concerned with the perception of things outside the self, but with passive being inside oneself, a state which is expressed most clearly in the definition of feeling given last, 'to wallow in feeling'. Feelings are, always, immediately-experienced 'qualities within the self or passive states in the self' (T. Lipps 1901; G. Anschütz 1953). They are something that the person who experiences them *is*, not something that he *has* (M. Krudewig 1947).

This passive character of feelings is shown particularly clearly in the permanent underlying temperament of a person. This basic temperament may be modified by many different influences. It cannot be separated from the physical state and is therefore dependent on all factors which influence this state; nourishment, temperature, climate, illness, physical exertion, drugs and so on. But a person's basic temperament is inborn and remains with him throughout his life.

The situation is quite different with the emotive moment of feeling. This is set in motion by a non-emotional experience, or, more precisely: an affection is only possible when the experience is linked with an emotion, a perception, or the grasping of a concept. Perceptions do not only give us objective information about the things in our environment; they either interest us, or bore us, or repel us. We are somehow touched by them, and we turn, not as spectators, but as participants towards the demands of the emotion, perception or concept which we have.

Listening to music is an activity which is said to be particularly suited to arousing emotion. Everyone must surely be aware that feeling is part of musical experience. Even the rationalist Descartes considered that 'the purpose of sound is to give us pleasure and to call forth different emotions' (1650, p. 1).

Thus it is not an accident that descriptions of the psychology of feeling begin with music (F. Krueger 1953), or that they favour examples from it (L. Klages 1934). Also it is surely not by chance that the German word '*Stimmung*' [English 'mood'] is borrowed from the realm of music to designate emotion.[1] Three of its characteristics bring music close to emotion: its basis in sensation, its unrelatedness to objective reality, and its subjectivity.

But this basis in sensation is not simply a limited sensual feeling: all the physical and intellectual sensations of the individual are focussed on the organ of perception. The farther the experience, perceptual or mental, is removed from the sensori-motor schemes, the weaker are the subjective emotional experiences in so far as these are based directly on sensori-motor schemes. Emotional experiences related to the world of objective reality are not excluded from it, but they lack the directness of sensory experiences and come in only as the world of objective reality is grasped through the intelligence: they are not attached directly to the sensory basis of the objective concept nor to the extension of this into its aesthetic manifestations.

Emotive feelings which are aroused by the experience of music are always linked with sensory perception. However complicated the melodic forms, however varied the harmonic or formal structure of a musical work may be, it never loses contact with the world of the senses. On the other hand, since it does not owe its existence to the world of objective reality, music is more inclined than anything else to arouse subjective emotion. In listening to music the thing which releases the affection 'objectively' is in fact, as was stated above, the attachment of sensations to an object. This is done by an outside stimulus but it takes place *inside* subjective experience, for these sensations have no existence outside the self.

This peculiar connection, both with the individual's inner world and with his physical sensations as perceived through his ears, together with the exclusion of the world of objective reality, account for the special place which music has in individual subjective experience – the only sphere in which the emotions can function.

1. '*Stimmung*' also means the tuning of an instrument.

6. Musicality

Musicality is the ability to experience music. In everyday speech this ability is considered to be a 'special ability', which is developed more strongly in some people than it is in others. Less musical people are not considered to be at a great disadvantage, because the ability to experience music, to criticise pieces of music, or to make music are not thought of as important and because many people think, wrongly, that other abilities have no connection with musicality.

Musicality is quite definitely not a 'special ability' unconnected with other fields of experience. The coincidence would be too great if it were by pure chance that the musical children always go too, when the more generally gifted pupils transfer from primary to grammar school [*Volksschule zu weiterführenden Schulen*]. Several investigations agree that musically gifted children have ability in other fields as well (V. Haecker and Th. Ziehen 1922). However, one cannot reverse the proposition, 'musical children are intelligent'. One cannot say: 'The unmusical child is not gifted in other things'. The truth is much more likely to be that the musical children are to be found within the large group of generally able children, but it is by no means impossible for a child who has gifts other than musical ones to be capable of little response to music. True unmusicality seems, however, to occur very rarely indeed (Feuchtwanger 1930).

Musicality, then, is not a 'special ability' but is the application of general abilities to music. The same abilities which enable a person to distinguish differences between noises, either of pitch or duration, enable him also to distinguish similar differences in music. On the other hand a lack of general ability is apparent also in relation to musical experience. For instance, an inability to think in more than one dimension makes an appreciation of harmony impossible.

Tests with educationally subnormal adults showed that, if dissonant tests were included in a series, the subjects were quite unaware of any difference between these and the sweetest harmonies that were played immediately before and after the dissonances. When one stops to consider it this result is no more surprising than the fact that a person who is deaf cannot hear music. Anyone who is utterly incapable of carrying out certain operations of intelligence cannot suddenly be found to possess these very same skills in relation to music.

It may therefore be assumed that success in the sphere of music would

45

go with similar achievement in non-musical fields. Achievement in music shows at least that success of a similar kind is possible in other fields too. From what has been said it is clear that an unlimited general ability is not always connected with musicality. Someone who deals particularly fluently with musical matters (which, by definition, are far from the world of objective reality), and who frequently indulges in this unobjective activity, will often show surprising clumsiness in dealing with practical matters. It is no accident that there is a shortage of artists who are both good musicians and good technicians.

All researches to date have confirmed that musicality should be understood as an inherited disposition to apply general abilities to the field of music. So its manifestations are as varied as are differences between people in general.

The ability to experience music is just as firmly woven into the total fabric of potential human abilities as the potential for understanding speech, for reading, for motor skills, and so on. Therefore the achievements and effects of musicality can only be considered as part of the total structure of human abilities.

2 · The Beginnings of Musical Experience in the First Year of Life

1. The General Development of the Child during the First Year

As soon as he is born the child has to begin to make certain adjustments to the decisive change in his environment. Now he is no longer protected by his mother's body, he has to get used to cold, to wet, light and noise; nourishment no longer flows uninterruptedly from his mother's bloodstream, but only comes to him at feeding times. During the first few weeks the new-born baby sleeps nine-tenths of the time.[1]

The movements of the newborn baby may be spontaneous, or they may be reflex responses to external stimuli. His instinctive reflexes are mostly limited to sucking. He is not yet able to distinguish different objects, but is only capable of general response to the impression made by the outside world on his sense organs. Taste, smell and hearing are present from the beginning but individual babies show considerable differences in the degree of stimulation which is required to provoke a response. As far as vision is concerned, the newborn baby is only able to perceive light and colour.

[1]. Remplein (1964) calls the first phase of early infancy, which lasts from five to eight weeks, 'the age of sleep'. The German writers on child development, unlike the English ones, give names to the stages into which they divide it. The 'age of awareness' succeeds the 'age of sleep'. This in turn is succeeded by the 'age of grasping' (Ch. Bühler 1931). She calls the first five months of life the 'age of looking', and Remplein refers also to the 'age of listening'. Griffiths (1954) in *The Abilities of Babies*, p. 27, notes the wide variation in approach among previous researchers into the development of very young children and remarks that Bühler (1930, 1935) omits all reference to speech development in the early months. The first speech item in her scale occurs at nine months.

'The emotional life of the newborn baby is still closely linked with the activity of the organs and the senses' (Remplein 1964, p. 176). 'Sensations such as hunger or sleepiness, which are determined by the state of the infant's body, are distinguished from "sensory feelings" like touch, smell, taste, vision and hearing, which are related to external stimuli'. The sensation may find direct expression in some kind of motor or reflex action. 'The most important characteristic of the emotional life of the newborn infant is the predominance of feelings of displeasure over feelings of pleasure'.[1] (Remplein 1964.)

This stage ends when the baby begins to smile, at about five to six weeks. This 'social smile' is an active response to the smile of his mother or of some other person who is close to him. It is quite different from the pursing of the lips that was observable from the first week, but which had no significance and which was simply a reflex action. It is with people that the infant usually first establishes a relationship, but this is quickly extended to things in his environment. 'The infant now starts to take in . . . impressions of external stimuli, and thus he begins to be capable of true perception, as opposed to mere sensation'. (Remplein 1964, p. 182.) However when an infant of this age perceives, he does so quite differently from an adult. The adult often perceives things in an objective way, or at any rate, he is capable of doing so. But in an infant of six to eight weeks perceptions and subjective emotions are still confused. He gives the objects which he perceives in his environment a personality or a life of their own, so much so that Kroh (1944, p. 89) uses the term 'physiognomic perception' [personalized] to describe the perception of an infant of this age. The baby listens to his environment, as well as watches it.[2]

Until about five months the infant's only contact with the outside world is through the senses. So Ch. Bühler (1931) calls this time 'age of looking'. Remplein also speaks of an 'age of listening'.

1. A. T. Jersild, *Child Psychology*, 6th edn 1968, p. 68, 'Many opinions have been offered and much research has been done on a child's early emotions, but unfortunately both the opinions and the research leave large questions marks. . . . It must be recognized that a child is helpless. . . . To say that a newborn child is capable of feeling loneliness, love and hate assumes a level of maturation that goes beyond what is known about the nervous system of a child at birth'.

2. K. Pech, *Hören im optischen Zeitalter*, 1969, 'Active listening, not just an involuntary action, but following a sound with interest, occurs earlier in a child's development than active seeing, that is during the first six months of life'.

About five months the infant is no longer content simply to look at and listen to his surroundings; he begins to grasp at objects, so that at this stage of development the most important of the senses is touch.

Signs of developing memory appear between the ages of six and nine months. The baby recognizes familiar people and answers their smile by smiling back at them; but to a stranger's smile he often responds by turning away and crying, quite a different reaction from his earlier behaviour. Since the appropriate memory image is lacking, he shows fear of strangers (Spitz 1960). What he perceives is related to a memory image, and the mental activity is set in motion by the perception. It is not a case of seeking something in the real world which corresponds to an image which already exists in the memory.[1]

About this time, when he has learned to distinguish his parents from other adults, he starts using the words 'Mummy' and 'Daddy'. By saying the name of the person he knows well, the baby clearly expresses in sound the fact that he has perceived someone whose image is stored in his memory. He also practises speech sounds in his babbling monologues, using his sense of hearing to check whether his speech apparatus is making the movements he wants it to make. Memory must be at work here, since the speech sounds are repeated. So from about nine months the function of the babbling monologues changes; the infant is no longer simply exercising his speech apparatus in a playful way. He also begins to babble to other people and to communicate with his environment by making speech sounds, and not simply by listening and smiling. He shouts to attract attention or babbles tunefully, repeating syllables like 'bab-bab' or 'dad-dad'.

The ability to match something perceived to a memory image, of which several examples have been given, is the source of all intellectual development. Between nine and twelve months there is also a considerable development of manipulative skills. The baby can now pick up small objects with his fingers and he begins to learn to feed himself. He may try to use his intelligence to recover a toy which is out of his reach, and draw it towards himself by using another object; but is by no means always successful at doing this. He deliberately drops toys out of his pram and watches them fall to the ground, and he may even try to retrieve

1. This is only one of the possible theories about the growth of perception. See K. Lovell, *An Introduction to Human Development*, 1969, chapter 3; also H. G. Furth, *Piaget and Knowledge*, 1969.

them by throwing another toy after them. He learns to sit up, to pull himself up, to crawl, to stand up and to walk, in that order, though children vary enormously in the age at which they develop these abilities. A 'normal' child can stand alone for a few moments by the time he is a year old.

2. The Beginnings of Musical Experience

During the last months of pregnancy, a mother not infrequently notices that when she listens to music or goes to a concert her baby is particularly active. Stirnimann (1940, p. 51) thinks that these reactions are caused by sensations of hearing in the foetus itself, but his researches did not exclude the possibility that the sensations of hearing were in the mother. The motor reactions may well be a sympathetic experience with that of the mother and be based on the sensations of hearing in the mother, and not in the child. It is not impossible that in the intra-uterine stage the baby possesses the faculty of hearing, as Stirnimann says he does, but since no detailed research has yet been done on motor reactions in the foetus in the presence of music, no firm conclusions can be stated, and one must simply take note of the fact that children often move violently within their mother's womb when music is played.

For the first few weeks after birth the baby reacts to any sudden loud noise with muscular contractions which are very similar to the movements provoked by music when the child is still in the intra-uterine stage (B. Lowenfeld 1927). When he hears certain soft sounds, for example the voice of his mother or nurse, he becomes restless and starts making typical searching movements showing that the instinct to suck has been aroused (Remplein 1965).

A reaction to specifically musical sounds cannot be observed until about the time of the baby's first smile. It is quite different from the strong reflex actions of the intra-uterine stage and the first few weeks of life, when the baby is startled by sudden loud noises. Music no longer arouses, but has a distinctly calming effect. All the lullabies which have been handed down for generations show how widely this reaction of babies has been exploited for centuries. The effect is even stronger if the baby is rocked or cradled at the same time; the rocking movement on its own without the singing has a calming effect, but when the two are added together the effect is doubly great.

However, not all movements calm an infant; jerky or quick movements are more inclined to wake the baby up, while the calming effect is produced only by the gentle swaying to and fro. It is tempting to try to relate this difference to the music, and to infer that slow music calms and quick music wakes up. This conclusion is to a certain extent justified, in that we ourselves know that lively rhythms may dispel fatigue, while slow long-drawn-out melodies may send us to sleep.

However, we cannot simply transfer this effect from ourselves to an infant without futher consideration. The newborn baby does not yet hear music as something that takes place within the mental present; which is essential if the rhythmic pattern, something that takes place in time, is to be perceived. The child of this age cannot yet notice any difference between successions of sounds at different speeds, so that for him music lacks the dimension slow–quick. So other songs as well as lullabies may serve to calm a baby.

The author's ten year old daughter, Ute, regularly sang several songs to her baby sister, Susanne, during the first few weeks of the baby's life while the infant was being bathed and changed. This always calmed the baby, even when she was screaming with hunger. If Susanne was lying restlessly in her cradle, Ute could always calm her with a song. The songs which Ute sang on these occasions were by no means always lullabies, but were mostly lively folk or traditional songs. These songs quieted the baby just as much as the lullabies did, but if the author sang something to his baby daughter the child was not soothed, or not so much as when her sister sang to her. Other fathers had the same experience with their children; and the reason most frequently given for this was that the infant was not familiar enough with the sound of his father's voice: the baby's mother, and his brothers and sisters, were with him all day; so he would have plenty of opportunity to get used to the sound of their voices. This explanation seems to make sense; however one must take into consideration the fact that the sound of a flute soothed the baby the very first time she heard it; and songs sung by Ute's friends, whose voices the baby had never heard, also soothed her. In neither of these two cases could there be any question of the baby being familiar with the sound.

At Christmas the mother of a large family noticed that there was an unexpected and pleasant side effect when they stood the Christmas tree on an old musical box, which played carols for five minutes with the Christmas tree slowly revolving on top of it. The baby, who was only a few weeks old, regularly fell asleep while this was going on. He did this so unfailingly that when the Christmas season was over he could not go to sleep without the musical box. There it stood, without its Christmas tree, beside the baby's cot and sent the baby to sleep quite regularly. Much to the amusement of friends and relatives this went on, the musical box playing '*O du fröhliche*' and '*Kling Glöckchen*'[1] until Shrove Tuesday. The parents thought that the reason why the musical box sent the baby to sleep was that it played the same carols more and more slowly, until their attention was drawn to the fact that the baby boy was asleep long before the tunes had noticeably begun to slow down. So it is no more likely that the soothing effect of music on an infant can be attributed to a slow speed, or slowing down, than it can to familiarity with the sound.

High-pitched voices and instruments seemed to soothe, and low-pitched voices did not have this effect even when the singer was someone in the baby's immediate environment, so that one can only suppose that the important factor is the frequency range. Clearly, sounds in the higher frequency range have a particularly soothing effect, whether the sound is strange or familiar (E. Walker 1927).

3. Earliest Signs of Active Responses to Musical Stimuli

The youngest children who were given the tests described in the introduction were five to six months old. On the few occasions when the test music was played to younger children there was very great difficulty in finding a time when the baby was awake but not otherwise occupied, since there was little time for systematic experiments when the baby was not either hungry, being fed, or being changed. So, even if the researcher did decide to play the musical tests to the baby, it was extremely difficult to decide whether or not anything had been grasped. In these cases the reports of parents' observations, and observations made outside the formal test situation, were particularly important in supplementing the results of the tests.

1. Two very well-known German Christmas carols.

The findings of the tests and observations may be summarized as follows. Between the fourth and the sixth months, in exceptional cases as early as the third month, the behaviour of infants when they hear music changes most noticeably. The baby is no longer calm and sleepy when he hears music; quite the contrary. He now listens to the music and turns towards the source of the sound stimulus, often with an unmistakable expression of astonishment. One particular small subject was lying in his mother's arms when the musical tests were played. He looked steadily at the source of the sound, and at the end of each test turned and looked up at his mother with wide open questioning eyes. Two other children behaved in the same way, looking at their mothers at first questioningly, and then giving a beaming smile. Many parents reported that their children listened attentively and then looked happily at the radio.

The unmistakable pleasure which even children of six months may show when music is played is a clear indication that even at this age music may cause an emotional experience, and that this is not simply a question of bodily feelings but has an affective character. But the affection is not related to a physiological need, like the appeasement of hunger or thirst, the removal of unpleasant dampness, or the giving of warmth; it is related to something which can only give pleasure because it has been perceived, and which fulfils no practical purpose. The expression of astonishment shows that this is a new and hitherto unknown experience – which marks the beginning of a distinction between what is useful and what is not necessarily so – while the only meaning which can be attached to the smile is that the baby has been touched by a pleasurable experience. The emotional effect is not diminished if the experience is repeated frequently, so the supposition that it is the element of novelty which gives the pleasure cannot be correct.

Some of the six months old subjects stopped what they were doing when the music sounded, turned towards the loudspeaker, and remained motionless. It is tempting to try to relate this leaving-off of an activity to the soothing and calming effect which music has on younger infants. However, there is a fundamental difference between the two types of behaviour. The calm of the earliest months of life was, for the most part, a passive state, an experience which could only be deduced from its result, while the standing still which has just been described involves actively shutting out other experiences and concentrating on the music. The fact that even at this age some children stop feeding and turn towards the music does not support a point of view which is commonly held – that physiological needs automatically take precedence over all others.

The exact age at which a child first shows a response to music varies greatly from one individual to another; it is hereditary differences in the rate of development which chiefly determine whether a child first perceives music actively at the age of four months or at the age of six months. The musical environment seems to play a much less important part, at least as far as the amount of music available is concerned. The amount of time each day when music was available varied greatly from one subject to another. The longest time was from eight to nine hours a day (including times when the baby was asleep); the shortest time was a mere five minutes a day. Surprisingly enough, this enormous difference in the quantity of the music presented does not affect the time at which the baby begins to show some response to the music that he hears. Whether differences in quality of the music heard affect the baby's response is something that would have to be determined by a separate investigation.

Several other transitional responses must be mentioned in connection with the change from passive receptivity to active perception of music heard. They cannot often be seen, since they may be observed at most for a day or two.

Some of the six months old subjects showed that they were approaching the stage of active listening by becoming restless when they heard music. With another group of infants music simply ceased to have a soothing effect. Finally, in the case of two of the children who were observed, the old way of responding and the new one went on at the same time. One infant suddenly opened his eyes wide and looked at his mother as she was singing the evening lullaby to him, and then began to suck his finger as usual and soon fell asleep. The other one, a four months old boy, blinked several times at his grandmother as she sang to him, and then fell asleep as usual.

The different series of tests varied in the extent to which they attracted the attention of those children aged about six months who did respond to music. The ones which attracted the attention of the children by far the most often were Series 1 (Nursery Songs) and 4 (Instrumental Music). The series of noises and also the rhythms (Series 3) hardly aroused any reaction. This is all the more surprising in that the rhythms were much louder than the other series of tests. On the other hand the dissonant Series 5 attracted more attention.

The remarkably strong attraction of Series 1 and 4 for the children could not be explained by pure chance, even from the point of view of numbers. The following summary shows some of the details:

If a subject responded to one series only, that one was always either the nursery songs or the instrumental music; if he responded to two series, then they were these same two. If more than two series of tests attracted the baby's attention, then songs and instrumental music were, in every case, among the tests to which he responded.

If a common factor is sought in the two series of tests which attracted the attention of the six months old subjects so strongly, this is found to lie, in both cases, in the noticeably sweet sound of the two series. In all the other tests the purely euphonious character of the sound is diminished by some other musical element. The six months old baby does not give his attention, either to music which has the greatest degree of intensity, or which has the richest rhythm. He ignores blaring sounds, and also sounds in which the element of speech is in the foreground. *His attention is given first and foremost to the sound itself.* Thus our research confirmed the findings of König (1903), who was the first to state that children first enjoy music for its sound, not for its rhythm or its words. Today we may go farther and say that the child does not respond indiscriminately to any musical sound, but that he responds by selecting the sensuously beautiful sound. Thus even the six months old baby is moved by beauty of sound.[1]

1. J. L. Mursell, *Education for Musical Growth*. Ginn, 1948, p. 30, 'There are strong reasons for believing that a young child's primary responsiveness to music is first and foremost the tone itself, and not, as is sometimes asserted without any good evidence, to rhythm or to melody. Of course, the remarkable calming effect of croonings and songs and lullabies is a matter of universal human experience. But there is more than this. Students of infant behaviour have pointed out that about the third month of life there appear in the vocal patterns very characteristic babblings and lallings that go on spontaneously. These are in effect, comfort sounds. They do not belong definitely in the category of either speech or song, but are the matrix out of which both develop, and they have an appreciable tonal content. It has been argued that such experiences and reactions are the original sources of what later becomes aesthetic pleasure in music and in the sheer sound of language. . . . Furthermore, investigations have indicated that during the pre-school and even the kindergarten period, the child is much more pre-occupied with the tonal content and appeal of music than with anything else about it . . . (Belaiew-Exemplarski 1926).

'Ultimate musical responsiveness, then, is organic, perceptual and emotional

4. The Earliest Movements in Response to Music

For a while the infant is content with a passive response to music.[1] But about the age of six months, when he begins to grasp small objects (Ch. Bühler 1928) and no longer simply looks at or listens to things around him passively, he begins to react to his surroundings by moving; he is increasingly able to co-ordinate the actions of his sense organs, with the sense of touch leading the way.[2] At this stage, a few weeks after he has first begun to respond to sounds by actively turning his attention to the source of them, the infant begins to respond with motor movements to music. He begins to move when he hears music, not in an unorganized, restless way, but with very clear repetitive movements. Many children sway to and fro or from side to side, while others bounce up and down. Movements of individual parts of the body are more rarely met with in infants of this age; they do not, for example, often beat regularly on the cot blanket or make 'conducting' movements, or kick both legs regularly.

The movements may be tentative or violent, according to the baby's temperament or the intensity of the particular experience. One subject was sitting on a rocking chair and soon after the music began he started to rock so violently that his father had to hang on to the chair to stop it falling over. With all the children a short pause was clearly observed while they simply listened attentively before starting to move. No child began to move straight away. If a child was occupied with some other sort of movement before the music started, he did not go on making the same movement rhythmically. That movement stopped while he listened to the music for a short time, and then the movement made to the music was quite different from the one which he had started to make before it began.

We had expected that the children would move most to the rhythmically strong music (Series 3); our expectations proved to be quite wrong. It was again Series 1 and 4 (Songs, and Instrumental Music) which provoked

---

response to tone itself. It is prepotent in the musical experience of the little child. It is the basic reason why music has a strong appeal for unsophisticated and untrained people. And highly sophisticated and musically trained persons are influenced by it far more than they sometimes recognize'.

1. It is the 'age of looking' (Ch. Bühler 1928) and the 'age of listening' (Remplein 1965).

2. Some babies show a good deal of motor activity at a much earlier age than six months. See K. Lovell, *An Introduction to Human Development*, 1969, p. 10.

the strongest response in movement. If a child accompanied other tests with motor movements this activity was always most marked in the series with songs and instrumental music. It seems particularly absurd that precisely those tests which were included in the series because of their strong rhythmic quality did not call forth any motor response, while songs and instrumental music released noticeably intensive and varied motor activity. The question must be asked whether the movements which were observed were, in fact, in response to the rhythmic element in music, or whether they were simply a release of energy triggered off by the sense impression (R. Spitz 1960), especially since the movements of children were not rhythmically coordinated with the music, nor in time with it.

The second of these two possibilities is the less likely, since it is not necessary to have 'beautiful' sounds for a release of energy to take place and there is no reason, either, why a pure release of energy should take the form of the regular swaying and swinging movements that were observed. Energy certainly is released in these movements that are made in response to music, but the way in which this happens shows that something more than a simple reflex is involved. Though the rhythm of the movements does not follow that of the music, and is not co-ordinated with it, the movements in response to music do follow typical patterns, which is not the case with movements in response to other auditory stimuli. So it is the impression made by the sound on the sense of hearing which sets off the response in movement. Yet the infant only begins to move after he has been listening passively for a short while; so he must, to a certain extent, be aware of a series of sounds in time, and not simply be responding to a completely vague impression of sound. It is just as unlikely that, since he has begun by being aware of the impression of the sound on his sense of hearing, he will suddenly start to take no notice of that impression, and simply respond to the rhythmic series of sounds with motor activity.

There are four reasons for considering the first responses with movement to music to be a response both to the element of pure sound and to the rhythmic pattern:

1. The sound and the rhythmic pattern can only be separated from each other by a process of abstraction. The infant cannot yet do this.
2. Every realization of music in dance takes into account the element of pure sound as well as that of rhythm. Is there any reason why this should not happen with the earliest movements to music?

57

3. The earliest movements to music are not synchronised with it. Yet, as well as a response to the sound, they may also be taken to be a subjective response to the rhythmic pattern since movements to music are usually determined more by the rhythm than by anything else.

4. Eventually these earliest movements to music develop on the one hand into very precise movements, rhythmically co-ordinated with the music, and on the other hand into motor responses which follow the climaxes, the phrasing, or the dynamics of the music, in the manner of modern educational dance.

These repetitive movements are the earliest form of musical response to include something more than simple perception. To sum up: though they are not synchronised with the music, they are rhythmical in themselves; they are a response both to the sound and to the rhythm, and so are surely related not only to the sound at a given moment, but also to the sequence in a short passage of music. So they must be taken as the beginning of a response to rhythm in music.

It is very difficult to say at exactly which stage in a child's development movements in response to music may begin. First, the times at which various abilities mature vary greatly from one individual to another, and secondly, a child may possess an ability for some time before an opportunity occurs for him to use it. Furthermore, the earliest tentative movements to music may remain unnoticed for a long time. It is, however, possible to give some indication of the time at which a child may begin to respond to music with repetitive movements, since the stage of pure 'listening' – that is turning attentively towards the source of the music – always precedes the stage of movement. Vocalizations in response to music only start *after* motor movements to music have begun to be made.

Thus the age at which a child first begins to move to music depends on the age at which he first begins to turn his attention towards it. So one would expect that the earlier the child begins to listen actively to music, the earlier he would begin to move to it. According to our observations responses in movement began anything from two to eight weeks after the first active listening. Because of the variation in this length of time, which is especially large for this early age, it is quite possible for children whose active listening has begun later, but whose response with movement has followed after only two or three weeks, to respond with rhythmical movements earlier than children who began to listen actively much earlier but who took their time over starting to respond with movements. Because these differences are so large, a response with movement to music may begin any time between the fifth and the eighth month. If an infant begins to turn his attention to music at an early age, and if the stage of 'active listening only' lasts for a short time, this does not necessarily mean that he is particularly musical, or, as far as we know at present, that he will develop a musical talent.

5. The Earliest Vocalizations to Music and Musical Babbling

Shortly after they begin to respond to music by moving, children begin also to respond by making sounds. We can distinguish two types of response: 1. Vocalizations, 2. Musical babbling.

The first group comprises two types of vocalization: first, the chuckling and 'crowing' of infants when they express pleasure, and secondly, the 'babbling monologues' in which they may show their enjoyment either during or after the performance of a piece of music. Most children show also a kind of serious surprise on hearing music. Depending on their temperament and their degree of courage small children who can crawl or even walk may either struggle to get to the radio or tape recorder, or keep a respectful distance from the source of the sound.

'Musical babbling' differs from both the previously mentioned types of response that show delight in sound. The term was first used by Schünemann (1930) to designate songs which were completely lacking in words. We use it to distinguish these sounds from the 'babbling monologues' which are the precursors of speech (K. Bühler 1930).

Babbling in preparation for speech begins as early as the second or third month of life; the speech sounds are practised, beginning with the vowels and proceeding from the easiest to those more difficult to articulate. The vowels are followed by the labial sounds, then the dentals and so on until 'r' and 'l', the most difficult sounds of all, are reached at the end of the babbling stage. In the course of these 'babbling monologues' one or two baby words, like 'dada' and 'nana', the sound '-ss' on its own, or a long drawn out 'n' appear. At first these baby words may relate to absolutely anything, but, as speech develops, one such word after another gets related to a particular class of people or objects and eventually comes to be used only in connection with specific people or things.

Musical babbling was not investigated by earlier researchers into the development of speech. It differs from speech babbling in that the speech sounds are not practised repetitively but sounds of most varied pitch are produced, either on one vowel or on very few syllables (Moog 1967). This still happens when the child has passed far beyond the very early playful practising of speech sounds and is already capable of forming most difficult ones. The clearest proof of the distinction between speech babbling and musical babbling is as follows: speech babbling is produced in the six or seven months old infant by talking to him; musical babbling only occurs if music is sung or played to him.

The tapes which were recorded of babbling songs did not show any clear pattern of development, as is the case with speech babbling. What they did show were certain characteristics of the singing of early infancy. These earliest vocalizations are not in any sort of diatonic system and are also rhythmically amorphous. The melodic lines are mostly descending, and if they do move upwards, this is usually by leap (W. Platt n.d.).[1]

The range of pitch of many infants is in fact surprisingly wide and unexpectedly low, being centred round f'. The tapes included examples showing that a number of children had a vocal range of more than an octave. Within this wide range of pitch the babbling monologues moved in microintervals (see Figure 1).

For this reason a special notation must be used in transcribing the tapes of the singing of infants. As well as the usual accidentals, we have indicated differences of pitch up to a quarter of a tone flatter with (♭) and up to a quarter of a tone sharper with (♯). For instance, the note indicated by

lies within the range g' and a quarter of a tone above g', while the note indicated by lies between A flat and a quarter

of a tone below A flat. All the transcriptions give the absolute pitch of the singing.

---

1. There can be no question of an 'original third' (i.e. *Urterz* in German) (W. Hansen 1952) a 'single tonic' (*Henotonik*) (D. Bruhn 1950) or a 'glissando on one tone' (*Eintonglissando*) (G. Kube 1958). See also G. W. Silverstolpe 1926 and H. Neugebauer 1929.

Figure 1. *Babbling songs of children aged eight months*

Babbling song no. 1

Babbling song no. 2

Babbling song no. 3

From the tests and observations which have been made to date, we found that the earliest vocalizations to music occurred at just six months and always came after the stages of pure listening and motor response. The fact that speech babbling begins two to four months before singing babbling, leads to the supposition that a child responds to music with some kind of vocalization expressing pleasure or with some kind of speech babbling before he begins to answer music with musical babbling. Unfortunately we could not record enough examples to justify the assertion that vocalizations expressing pleasure or speech babbling precede musical babbling.

One more fact in connection with the development of speech ought to be mentioned: speech babbling begins before musical babbling, but the child sings his earliest babbling songs before he can say his first word.

The following table shows the percentage of subjects who responded to the test with musical babbling, and the percentage of children who vocalized in response to music but did not actually sing.

Figure 2. *Vocalizations to music, including babbling songs of children up to the age of two years*

Age Year, Month	Vocalization to music, not including babbling songs	Vocalization to music, including babbling songs and singing	Total
0.3	5%	0%	5%
0.6–0.7	15%	15%	30%
0.8–0.9	50%	50%	100%
0.11–1.1	40%	60%	100%
1.5–1.7	10%	90%	100%
1.11–2.1	0%	100%	100%

The shift in the percentage of the two groups of children's vocalizations to music, as is clear from the table (Figure 2), supports the theory that children make some kind of vocalized response before they are capable of babbling songs. However, this table does not provide conclusive proof because we did not observe other kinds of vocalization from all the 'singers', and it is quite possible that those children who did make some sort of vocalization to us, as well as babbling tunefully, may have begun these vocalizations before they began to produce babbling songs.

Apart from a few exceptions, the songs of children before the age of one year bear no resemblance to what is sung or played to them. They do not copy the rhythm, the pitch, or even the direction of a melody; and the speech sound of the words is not imitated either.

6. The Effect of the Emergence of Memory on Musical Experience

By the age of nine months children of normal development have passed the stage of simply listening passively to music and of responding to it with motor movements and are now able to make some sort of response in sound. Half of the children whom we observed made a most distinctive sort of response in sound, which may be called musical babbling. The number of all three kinds of sound response increases amazingly quickly between the age of six months and one year. The total extent of this increase cannot easily be determined, as each response to music is both longer and more intense. About the age of nine months a noticeable increase in the quality, as distinct from the quantity, of response begins to appear. For the first time the child is able to express dislike and distaste as well as joy and pleasure on hearing music. Furthermore at this stage the child makes his first attempts to talk and these too have an effect on musical experience.

These two new forms of response may be traced back to a common source which has already been mentioned, namely the beginning of the operation of memory.

Up to the age of nine months the infant can show signs of displeasure only in relation to bodily states. He can react to music only by enjoying its pleasant sounds and accepting it, or by ignoring it; ugly sounds merely go unnoticed. But at nine months the earliest signs of rejection, displeasure and distaste on hearing music appear. Some subjects gave a clear indication of rejection simply by turning away from the source of the sound. Other children, while not actually turning away, quite definitely pulled a face at the sound. One little girl, after looking at it disgustedly for a while, called out in a rage: 'Hi'. Another little girl of nine months, who was exceptionally forward with talking, made the comment 'On' to Series 5 (Cacophonies). This meant that she wanted to hear more of it. Instead of repeating this series we played the noises, Series 6. She responded to this with 'On? – No! – 'fraid' [afraid], and ran to her mother as fast as her wobbly little legs would carry her.

With a few exceptions (one subject showed that he rejected Series 2) the series which provoked most signs of rejection were numbers 3 and 6 (Pure Rhythms and Noises). These two series are clearly the ones which do not present beautiful sounds. It was astonishing to see how two children, besides pulling faces, babbling, and making the usual repetitive movements to Series 3, showed their dislike of the sound. Clearly the sensuously ugly element in this series provoked a different response from the purely rhythmic element.

In considering changes in the quality of response to music, it must also be noted that some of the children aged eight to nine months responded more strongly to Series 2, because they were beginning to be aware of language and able to pay attention to the sounds of speech. A few children showed strong motor reactions to the series of 'Words with Rhythm' but remained completely impassive to Series 3, the 'Pure Rhythms'. The behaviour of these children can be explained only by assuming that it was the speech sounds of the tests which first attracted their attention, and that they then went on to respond to the rhythmic element; so it may be assumed that children respond differently to the different elements in the tests. Since children of this age are beginning to be aware of language we found a few, though very rare, instances of some sort of similarity between what is played to the children and what they themselves sing in their musical babbling. These songs bear no resemblance whatever either to the pitch or to the rhythm; they simply have *a faint likeness to the sound of the words*. In all the cases where this similarity was observed, it

Fig. 3 Song of a ten months old child to the song 'The Gay Tyroleans'.

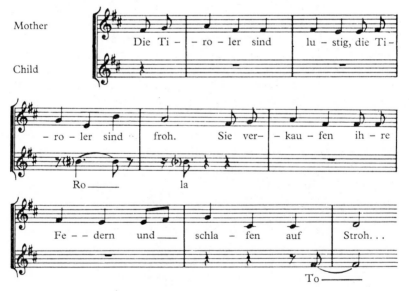

only occurred after the songs had been sung to the child many times, and always in the form of an accompaniment. The example given in Figure 3 is the transcription of a response of this kind to 'The Gay Tyroleans'. The ten months old child had been babbling musically for some time, but this was the first occasion on which his parents could distinguish any sort of resemblance to what was sung to him.

We heard babbling songs of this kind not only in response to nursery songs, but also to parts of Series 2, that is tests in which the speech element predominated.

Finally, a child may begin to show signs of using memory when he makes a movement he has been taught previously to a particular song. The best known of these – at least in the Rhineland – is the song 'Like the little flag on the tower', to which the adult makes a circling movement with his arm. During the last three months of their first year many children, if they have had enough practice at doing this to the music, are able to make this movement. If the song is sung to him the child starts to make the movement, and he still makes it if the song is not sung but the words are simply spoken rhythmically. This behaviour pattern confirms what was clear from other observations and tests, which may be summarized as follows:

The child's response to music during his first year of life is based entirely on the quality of the sound itself; but it soon begins to include an awareness of the rhythmic motor element and towards the end of the first year its development is hastened by awareness of the sound qualities of speech. Children of one year do not distinguish differences in pitch in melodic lines. The total sound, including its clarity, is taken in, but this clarity is not perceived in relation to the clarity of other sounds. No child under one year noticed the absence of definite pitches in the nonsense-word rhythms, and no child showed the slightest attempt in his own babbling songs to keep to the pitch of what was sung to him. So one essential element in the perception of melody, the awareness of differences in pitch, is not yet present in a child aged one year.

3 · The Musical Experience of the Child from One to Two Years

1. The General Development of the Child between the Ages of One and Two

The best known authorities on child development all agree that a most important change takes place about the time of the child's first birthday, as he begins to learn to walk and to talk (Osterrieth, Piaget *et al.* 1956; Bergius 1959). All living creatures except for a few of the lowest species, propel themselves along, but man is unique in that he does so in an upright position. Portman (1958) goes on to argue that it is this ability to stand upright, rather than the ability to propel himself in this position, that distinguishes man from the rest of the animal kingdom. Certainly the ability to walk has important consequences for a child's future development (Allport 1958). In order to walk, the child has to master the most delicate co-ordination of his limbs and the balance of his whole body, but, once he is able to stand up and walk around, his view of his immediate surroundings is quite different from what it was when he could only lie or sit. Once he can walk, he sees the world in an everchanging perspective and the range of possibilities is immeasurably greater.[1]

The acquisition of language has an equally revolutionary effect. However, well before his first birthday the child has been preparing for language by his babbling, an activity which is specifically human since no animal engages in it. These babbling words are most expressive, and the child's jabbering is usually related to some physiological process or to some

---

1. R. Griffiths, *The Abilities of Babies*, 1954, p. 14, notes that a rapid development of manipulative skills is possible once the baby has learnt to walk in an upright position, and his hands are freed from the need to help him creep and climb.

particular emotion. Between nine months and a year the child begins to be able to replace some of these babblings with proper word forms. But these early words, like the babbling words which they replace, are still an expression in sound of feelings, of subjective needs or wants. They simply serve to express the child's mood or state of excitement.

During the second year of his life, the child becomes increasingly able to give names to people, things and events as he learns that language can give names to things; and these things are no longer subjective states within the child himself but objects which he perceives in his environment. Even though these 'objects' are invested with strong emotional overtones by a small child, the ability to name people, things and events represents an important step out of the narrow egocentric world of the self into the world outside; he reaches out into the world by talking at about the same time as he takes his first walking steps into that same world.

2. The Amount of Response to Pieces of Music Played

Between the ages of nine months and a year a marked extension of musical response may be seen. There is an increase of about 20 per cent in the number of responses to music, in movement, in songs and utterances in response to the music played. This increase takes no account of differences in quality of response. However, this still does not give a true indication of the full extent of this increase, for not only is the number of responses greater but each action lasts noticeably longer; whether the children are simply taking notice of the source of stimulus or are responding to the music with movements or with singing.

Moreover, at the beginning of the second year children experience music more intensively than they did a few months earlier. Their attention cannot be so easily distracted from music once they have become aware of it, their movements to music have become larger and stronger, a fact observed so widely that it cannot be explained entirely by the general growth of motor ability at this age. It would not be difficult to devise a method of measuring the duration of individual responses to music, but a method of measuring the intensity of the experience has not so far been discovered. Yet we must take intensity into account as well as number and duration of responses, and consider it as an important factor in the increase in the amount of response to music. As with the duration, the energy used in a response could only be estimated, not measured exactly, with the methods available for this investigation. Since the number of responses to music at this age can be shown to have increased by 20 per cent, and the duration and intensity of each individual response have also clearly increased, the 20 per cent increase in the amount of response to music can only be considered as a base, to which certainly two essential additions must be made, that cannot yet be fixed quantitatively.

At this age, while the amount of response to music increases to the extent which has just been indicated, the number of children who show displeasure when music is played to them decreases. Half of the subjects aged nine months reacted 'negatively' to some tests. At the beginning of the second year only 33 per cent of the children turned away from the source of stimulus, cried, ran to their mothers or 'pulled a face'. 'Pulling a face' is at the same time an expression of displeasure and a protection against the music. It is related to the process of turning away from the source of stimulus, only in this case the child puts up with the sound for a moment.

Thus we frequently find the two following on each other, so that 'pulling a face' may, after a while, be followed by turning away. Two children responded to Series 5 and 6 with 'grumbling' and 'scolding'. With this sort of behaviour the question is no longer one of seeking protection or fleeing from the sound, it is not even a question of putting up with the sound, but of actively rejecting it. This sort of behaviour could not be observed in younger children.

The attitude of the children to the music played has also become clearly more positive. Not only did the number of 'negative' responses diminish by a sixth, but the babies began increasingly to react to ugly sounds not simply by seeking protection or running away, but by putting up with them and, in a few cases, even actively rejecting them. The sharp increase in the number of responses of all kinds slows down between the ages of twelve and fifteen months, and then a decline begins. Fifty subjects aged eighteen months showed a total of 455 active responses to the same tests to which 41 subjects aged one year responded with 469 actions. Taking into account the different number of subjects, the decline in the number of active responses between one year and eighteen months is over 20 per cent. If the number of responses in movement, per child of one year olds, is compared with that of children of eighteen months then the decline is as high as 25 per cent. The decline in the total number of song responses is still more noticeable, since the number of children who responded by singing showed a sharp rise at the same age.

This surprising result presented some problems when it came to evaluating the results of the experiments. How could there be an abrupt falling off in the number of responses to music at a time when the general development of a child makes rapid progress? The size of his vocabulary increases, and the child's motor development progresses at a greater rate than at almost any other stage in his life. Was musical experience to be proved to proceed differently from other development, contrary to the principle underlying this research?

The fear that a surfeit of music from the mass media might result in a turning away from music at this age proved unfounded. Children who, according to what their parents said, were exposed all day to radio, TV or records, showed no significant difference in musical development from the children who heard only five minutes of music a day. However, certain observations made it doubtful whether there really was a true decline in the development of responses to music. First, there were the reports of the parents of those children who had showed no response at all to the whole series of tests. Some of these had, a short while before, noticed their babies beating time to pop songs; one father had even observed the earliest sign of co-ordination between the music and his baby's movements. Other parents reported that their babies often wanted to join in singing games like 'Ring-a-ring-a-roses' and so on. All of these were types of behaviour which indicated that, as far as their musical development was concerned, these children were not below average.

A comparison of the different actions made in response to the musical tests strengthened the suspicion that the decline in the number of actions observed did not represent a real decline in musical development. With the one year old subjects, where the total number of movements was 25 per cent greater, the average difference of movement was 2.3 per subject. With the subjects aged eighteen months, although the total number of movements was fewer by one quarter, each subject taken individually showed 2.4 variety of response in movement to the music played. These two sets of figures on their own show only small evidence of progress. However, if the decline in the total number of movements is taken into account, and the number and variety of movement are correlated with each other a shift of 28 per cent in the relationship between variety and number of movements is seen to take place between the ages of a year and eighteen months.[1]

This proves conclusively that musical development is not out of step with general development. On the contrary, the marked growth in motor skills which is evident in children of this age shows itself also in response to music, both in the size and strength of individual movements and in the increase of about 28 per cent in variety of movement. But the proof that response to music is in step with general development was traced back to a hidden growth – in the variety of movement – not initially apparent, and not to a decline in the number of movements observed. This decline is due to an important step forward in the general development of children. Such a marked falling off in the number of responses observed could not be due to pure chance, and, as every series of tests was affected, as more or less all the children showed this surprising apparent decrease in their response to music, and as this group of subjects was not different from the others in any way, the cause could only be taken to lie in a fundamental change in general development.

An explanation may be found in the development of the child's ability to think. Until about the beginning of the second year the child's thinking is always based on immediate perceptions. Memory images are only brought into play if they are called up by actual perceptions. Piaget (1948) does not find evidence of mental processes based on other than immediate perceptions until about the age of fifteen to eighteen months. Piaget speaks of 'inner combinations', meaning the ability to represent to oneself

---

1. If the total number of the one year olds is taken as 100 per cent, then that of the children aged eighteen months is only 75 per cent. But since the variety of movement among the one year olds was 2.3 and among the children aged 18 months was 2.4 the relationship between variety and relative number of movements to music was 2.3 and 2.4, or, expressed as a percentage:

$$\frac{\dfrac{2.3}{100}}{\dfrac{2.4}{75}} = \frac{X}{100}.$$

relationships between things which are remembered, without the help of an actual perception.[1]

However, the thought process is always started by some perception or other. Until this stage the child was only capable of hearing music as a direct sensory experience and of responding with movements or with 'singing'. He could relate a sound which he heard with an image in his memory, such as calling out 'bow-wow' if he heard a dog barking. Most responses in movement or with sound were the result of the direct sensory experience, as the child was not yet able to internalize sound in his memory and still needed this direct contact with a sensory experience. All these responses were observable to the examiner, whether it was a question of turning towards the source of the sound, of making some response by moving or by 'singing', or of recognizing some music which had been heard before.

Once he is able to internalize actions, and to think, the child can use his sense impressions in the process of 'inner combination', and so some of his response is of a kind that cannot be observed. To sum up, the transition from the stage of sensori-motor intelligence to the stage of pre-operational thought affects the number of observed responses to music in two ways:

1. A musical perception may call up a memory image and this may set off a further train of 'inner combination'. If this happens the subject may not necessarily turn towards the source of stimulus, or show any outward sign of response that could be noticed by the examiner.

2. When one of the test pieces of music begins, the child may still be occupied with another chain of 'inner combinations' that are based on other sense impressions. As soon as the brain is engaged in thought, motor movements play a much less important role and sense impressions are not so easily ascertainable. It may be assumed that the young child, like the adult, economises his mental resources in this way, and if his mind is occupied with non-musical things he does not even perceive a musical test.

1. See K. Lovell, *An Introduction to Human Development*, 1969, p. 26, '. . . for the infant can increasingly represent to himself the various possible actions and how they must be combined, in order to attain some desired end. His actions are carried out in inward form; he has a flow of ideas directed to some end or purpose. In short, actions have become internalized and he is beginning to think'.

There is a difference between the two possibilities which have just been described. In the first case the music was experienced, but because of 'internalisation' this could not be observed. In the second case there was no experience of music at all, since the subject was occupied with other thoughts; so, again, no musical response was observable.

Neither of these instances of absence of an obvious response to music is a sign of a regression; on the contrary, both are clear indications of an essential advance in a child's development. It is impossible to say with certainty how much less music is in fact perceived, since the number of responses is small. What is certain is that a further, decisive, development of musical experience is made possible by the growth of logical thought.

3. Movements to Music

a. *Types of Movement*

Children aged two went on making only three of the movements which were typical of children aged six months; these were: rocking from side to side in a sitting position, bouncing up and down by moving the spine, and 'conducting'. But the frequency with which the different types of movement occurred was different among the two year olds from what it was with the children aged six months. 'Conducting' movements which were made relatively rarely by the younger children were now made three times as often as bouncing up and down and rocking from side to side. The exact form of these movements is different too, as the child can now stand up and walk about, from what it was when he could only lie down or sit up. He no longer stretches and bends his body by a movement of the trunk, but does it by bending the knees. Similarly, when he sways from side to side he does it by shifting his weight from one leg to the other hardly moving the trunk at all. Some of the children stood and swayed backwards and forwards to the music. When they did this most of them held on to something and tilted the whole body from the feet as they rocked to and fro, only moving the hips slightly. If the child has something firm to hold on to he jumps off the ground with both feet and stamps as he does so. With children of this age we did not observe this movement at all from a sitting position, though younger children make it so frequently. On the other hand, a movement such as 'conducting', which occurs relatively infrequently in younger children, appears three times as often in the one to two year old age group as the rocking and bending movements together.

As soon as children can stand and walk well enough they begin to spin round to music, singing babbling songs to themselves as they do so. The movement is soon extended into going round in a circle. This marks an important step in the development of movements to music, as the child now begins to use space in his responses. The two movements become linked to each other some time between the ages of eighteen months and two years. Children then turn round as they walk, making regular dance movements. This form of movement was the commonest of all among the children aged eighteen months; more than half of the subjects of this age made movements of this kind.

Besides these 'stepping' movements, there were a whole number of odd movements of parts of the body, which were observed anything between one and four times among the 100 subjects aged between one and two. All these movements were repetitive. The forms are listed below:

Seesawing with one foot
Nodding the head
Swaying the head from side to side
Raising and lowering the heels
Moving the knees backwards and forwards
Swinging one leg backwards and forwards
Kneeling and rocking from one knee to the other
Opening and closing a hand regularly.

About the age of eighteen months a few children begin to move to music in an entirely different way. They no longer perform the movements on their own but try to carry out their dance movements with a grown-up, or a brother or sister, or in a few cases even with a teddy or a doll. This is more than a variant of forms of movement already familiar to the children; it clearly shows a natural desire to carry out dance movements in company with another person (K. Blessinger 1929).

It would be a mistake to conclude that this marks the beginning of a child's wish to move to music in company with someone else. Usually, even before a child can walk he likes to be picked up and danced with, to music. But when this happens the child does not make the movements himself, or try to make them correspond in any way with those of his partner; it is much more a question of the mingling of two desires: to be rocked, and for physical contact with a familiar person. However, when children aged eighteen months onwards include another person or a doll in their dancing the observer is left in no doubt that, this time, he wants to dance with someone. This activity of children may therefore be taken to be the earliest sign of social behaviour in movement to music.

b. *Earliest Co-ordination of Music and Movement*

Another important sign of progress in movement to music occurs during the second year. Until the age of about eighteen months, unless a child has exceptional musical talent, one cannot take it for granted that the movements which he makes will correspond with the rhythm of the music played to him, even for a short stretch at a time. If the music changes from a slow to an obviously much quicker speed, a child will make some sort of quicker movement; but he is still not capable of making anything like a co-ordinated movement with the rhythm of the music.

Sometime between the ages of eighteen months and two years about ten per cent of children begin, for short stretches of time, to match their movements to the rhythm of the music. Clearly the young child experiences considerable difficulty in co-ordinating his movement with a series of musical sounds. The few children who are able to do this at all, are only able at first to keep up the co-ordination for a few bars at a time. The difficulty must surely lie in the child's inability to isolate the time element in the sounds which he hears, for until he begins to have some awareness of the passage of time he cannot begin to co-ordinate two such totally dissimilar elements as the sound of music and the movements of dancing.

The question is not simply one of relating either a simple succession of sounds or a simple succession of movements, but of relating the two series, sounds and movements, to each other; and since, as far as the music is concerned, it is only the series of sounds that is important, and all other elements in the music must be ignored, so also with movement: the use of space is unimportant and only the time element has to be considered. Thus the problem is to bring into relationship with each other one aspect of two quite disparate sensory fields, and, clearly, this cannot be done purely by processes of thought; it also involves action. Considering the magnitude of the difficulty which has to be overcome before a child can achieve this, his ability to match his movements to the rhythm of music must be regarded as a most important step forward in his development.

4. Songs

a. *Babbling Songs*

Figure 2 on p. 62 shows how the number of singers, which at the age of one year was about 60 per cent of the subjects, rises sharply during the next six months so that by the age of two every child of normal development can sing. But this increase makes no difference to the overall trend, which is a decrease in the total number of songs observed. It provides on the other hand even clearer evidence of children's growing intellectual development, since the smaller number of songs observed is shared among a considerably larger numbers of 'singers'.

Between the age of one and two there is a marked advance in spontaneous singing. Between the ages of eighteen months and two years many children no longer sing short phrases only, but manage longer songs. Habits of singing may be noticed: for instance some children sing regularly when they wake up in the morning; others during the day, when they are playing with a particular toy, running about the house, going for a walk, or before going to sleep. Many children link their singing with movements, as has already been described; others sing to themselves without making any movements. Words are not usually used in spontaneous singing between the ages of one and two but single words or parts of words may occur, scattered around in a string of nonsense syllables or at the beginning of a babbling song which after beginning with the word continues with the repetition of a single syllable. There is marked progress in the intervals which children use in their singing, since the number of microtonal figures declines noticeably towards the end of the second year. So the total effect is much nearer to the diatonic system.

In the very first babbling songs there are many microtonal figures such as several intervals smaller than a semitone within the range of a tone; intervals of roughly a third, a fourth, or a fifth occur. The examples which have been transcribed show that the 'good impression' rests mainly on the decline in the number of these microtonal figures, though in other ways the choice of intervals in the spontaneous singing of one to two year olds still bears little relation to the diatonic system. So the transcription can be given more or less correctly only if the extra signs for accidentals are used.

To reproduce the rhythm of children's songs no special notation is required, because our rhythmic notation is capable of representing all the rhythms which children use. Their songs are rhythmically very simple, and a number of those which we recorded used only notes of the same length. Most spontaneous songs show notes of two lengths, in the ratio of 1:2. Most of the time the shorter of these was used, the one which was twice as long only rarely. Only a small number of songs used notes of three or four different lengths, and the 'extra' notes only occurred in isolated instances, so they did not affect the fundamental principle, which was the domination of the whole song by notes of the same length. So it is safe to make the general statement that, from the age of eighteen months, children's spontaneous songs are dominated by one single note-length. This rhythmic simplicity is probably due to the children's very limited sense of time, which allows the singer to do little more than find his way from one note to the next.

However, this rigidity does not occur in the rests between the individual phrases of a song. The length of the rests is most varied and their duration is not related in any simple way to the length of note used. The following explanation may be offered for this: when the child sings he brings a rhythmic order into action; however, the rests between the individual phrases of a song do not represent any action for the child; so he cannot perceive them. Thus the length of the rests depends on the breathing of the little singer and his possible need to sing a bit more. The number of notes in a phrase is most varied, in contrast to the use of a single note value; phrases of two, three or four notes occur with a long note at the beginning, in the middle or at the end. There is no recognizable order in the arrangement of syllables or in the distribution of accents.

However, even though the songs of children aged one to two keep to notes of the same length, they are not necessarily always monotonous.

Figure 4. *Two spontaneous songs of children aged one to two*

Babbling song no. 1

Babbling song no. 2

b. *Songs Which Resemble Something Sung to the Child*

Some of the songs of children as young as one year may be shown to resemble something which has been sung to the child. However, only six per cent of the children on whom our research was based were capable of this kind of imitation.

In two cases we were lucky enough to observe the very first occasion on which a child produced a song resembling the model sung to him. The parents at any rate had not noticed this ability before. In these two cases, and with a few other one year olds, it was only the sound of some of the words of the song that was imitated. In one case this was restricted to the vowels of some words. The rhythm was not imitated at all.

Two children sang the vowels of 'Ding, ding, dong, dong', from Test Series 2 when it was played to them again, but they did not keep to the pitch of the spoken melody and were completely independent in their choice of interval. One child prattled away to himself while the test was being played to him; after hearing it he brought 'Ding, dong' into his babbling monologue at the corresponding place. Another child of nearly eighteen months brought 'Ding, dong' into a babbling monologue, which was hardly interrupted the whole time Test Series 2 was being played.

One little girl said only the word 'Tyroleans' after the playing of the song 'The Gay Tyroleans'. In neither of these two cases was the rhythm of the words, as given in the test, imitated. Only one child, aged just over a year, imitated the rhythm as well as the sound of the words, but it was not possible to discover whether it was this child's first attempt at imitating something sung to him; he could well have already passed the stage of imitating the sound of the words. With this exception, children at the start of their second year could only keep up the imitation of speech for a short time. This observation was confirmed by numerous reports from parents.

In a few rare cases the words were articulated more clearly and their rhythm also was imitated.

If we ask which words or parts of words the child sings first, we get the surprising answer that it is not necessarily the words with whose meaning the child is most familiar. This is what would have seemed most likely, since one would have thought that the child would be particularly orientated towards language when learning to talk. In actual fact, the words which the children chose to imitate first from the large collection of musical stimuli which our tests offered them were words with a distinctive sound pattern, for instance 'Tyroleans' or words which besides having a strong sound pattern were repetitive, like the babies' own earliest words, such as mama, tata and papa. 'Ding, ding, dong, dong', from Test Series 2, was used particularly often in this way.

The reason why children usually do not imitate pitch and rhythm first, but choose words or parts of them, is that speech sounds make a much greater impression on their senses than pitch or rhythmic patterns. The sound of speech, with the range of colour of the vowels and the combinations of sounds in the consonants, has such a powerful impact on the senses, compared with the evenness in pitch and timbre which is all that the spectrum of instrumental sounds can offer. How much speech brings to the total sound impression may be shown by the attempt to perform a recitative on an instrument. Such a rendering seems pale and boring. But the richness of the impression made on the senses by speech has its negative side as well.

Speech sounds cannot provide the building material for melodies in the same way as primary sounds of fixed pitch. The individual musical tone produces a weaker impression on the senses. This must be so: otherwise it could not be used to form the unit for building a melody, which is an arrangement of sounds of different pitches. Neither is rhythmic shape on its own a powerful stimulus to the senses; the sensory element must be incorporated into it in time.

When he begins to try to sing, the child does not give his attention to something that produces a poorer impression on the senses; so he takes notice first of speech sounds, which make the strongest impression. It may be objected that it is not, strictly speaking, speech which catches the child's attention, since he first imitates words whose meaning he does not yet know or which have no meaning. This objection would hold good for adults, since it is the symbolic function of speech which distinguishes it on the one hand from noise and on the other hand from music. However, even for adults, speech is not simply a tool for conveying meaning subject to the laws of logic. It is also a formation of sounds, which must be measured according to the laws of aesthetics, and for an adult too language is the expression of another human personality which he may like, fear or respect.

As soon as we hear a foreign language which we do not understand at all the function of conveying meaning ceases to be the main, central purpose of speech. We are then in the same position as young children.

We take what is said as an expression in sound of the personality of the foreigner and – since we are unable to grasp any meaning – we give our whole attention to the sound of the words. Adults, too, on listening to a completely strange language will not remember the most meaningful words but those with the most striking sound structure, and they will be able to repeat these if they can manage the correct articulation.

The small child is in an exactly parallel situation and reacts to speech sounds in precisely the same way. If the child was not capable of focussing his attention on speech images he did not understand, he would always be driven back on the few words which he did already know. It is only because he is receptive to speech sounds in general, and particularly to those which have a powerful effect on the senses, that he begins to amass the store of formants which must be acquired before speech can be filled out with meaning (K. Buhler 1930).

This capacity for paying attention to the sensory quality of sound provides the child with the raw materials of speech when he begins to learn to talk. When he begins to learn to sing it appears also in the tendency to imitate first the sounds of speech.

Since children can reproduce sounds of speech before those of different pitch or rhythm, we must conclude that they find the latter more difficult than the former.

Among the subjects aged eighteen months 90 per cent were singers (see Figure 2, p. 62). A good third of these sang something similar to what was sung to them. The ability to imitate something heard had become so fixed between the ages of a year and eighteen months, that the rhythm of the words as well as their sound was reproduced in something like the form of the original, even if it was not entirely correct. A good half of the 'singers' showed some similarity of pitch as well.

Twelve per cent of the subjects aged eighteen months either sang to 'la' or hummed something approaching the rhythm and the pitch of the model. With four per cent of these children this did not mean that they ignored the words, since their parents had not sung words to them but had simply sung to 'la', which thus took on the function of words.

Eight per cent of the subjects aged eighteen months, however, contrary to the general trend, approached the problem of repeating something sung to them not by imitating the sound of the words, but by approximating the rhythm and the pitch to what had been sung.

All 'similar' songs which were 'sung back' had this in common: they were relatively short. This is equally true when, during a babbling monologue or musical babbling, short stretches of the test music just played are included. However, we also observed children who only listened to the beginning of the song sung to them and then sang one or another word from the test as it was being played. Even gifted children did not keep up their imitation for more than a few bars at a time.

Without exception the children never sang these songs after hearing them only once, as they would if following a leader. All the children had heard the song more than once, in most cases three or more times, before beginning to sing. The earliest attempts at imitation came at the second hearing, when one or two vague sounds were produced. One child imitated the sound of the words at the second hearing. With all the other children the examiner did not notice any similar phrases until the fifth repetition. Most of the songs used in the tests were already well-known to the children; consequently the number of times a child aged one to two must hear a song before he can imitate it must be much greater than the number which we counted.

Again and again we noticed that children waited for the end of a test, and then tried to sing a snatch of what they had heard. Strictly speaking, each time a child sings during a test he is, in fact, imitating it. This is obvious when children sing after hearing a song. When children sing with a song when it is repeated, the repetition has clearly given them the stimulus to join in but they have the added difficulty of trying to fit the bits which they know into the right place. That they do not always quite succeed is clear from the transcription in Figure 5, p. 81, where the child joins in too soon. The dominating influence of the words when children imitate a song is shown in the following ways:

1. By far the greatest number of 'imitating songs' show word co-ordination.
2. If snatches of the melody and the rhythm are imitated, as well as the words, the imitation of the words is always better than that of the rhythm and the pitch.
3. In all cases in which similarities of words and rhythm could be established, the rhythm imitated always followed the text.
4. No children of eighteen months were able to keep to the pitch or the rhythm of a song for more than a bar at a time. Only word imitation could be kept up for longer than a bar, and only four per cent of the children could do this.

Figure 5. *Songs of children aged one to two years*

Mother

Hop – pe, hop – pe Rei – ter

Child, after a
short pause

Hop – pe hop – pe hop – pe hop – pe

and after another short pause

Hop – pe, hop – pe

Mother. End of 'Little John.'

. . .eilt nach Haus ge – schwind.

Child sings it back in
microintervals.

i ö hö hö hö

Children aged eighteen months were less successful at imitating rhythm, and this sort of imitation occurred much less frequently than imitation of words. Fewer children tried to imitate rhythm, and those who did try did so less frequently than they tried to imitate words. Easily the most successful attempts at imitating rhythm were those where the rhythm was combined with the sound of a word, or with another noticeable sound pattern such as a calling figure or otherwise significant turn of phrase.

Only about half the children who were able to imitate words were also able more or less to repeat differences of pitch in melodies which had been sung to them. The following points about the imitation of pitch differences were noticed:

1. In a few cases it was only the direction of the melody which was followed.
2. Often snatches of melody were repeated with smaller intervals. (See transcription, Figure 5.)
3. In other cases the exact intervals were given in a sort of parallel form either with the song, or after it. For instance the interval sung was nowhere near the third, fourth or fifth of the model.

4. A few children succeeded in repeating the exact pitch for as long as a whole bar, but they were only able to do this if they were singing a repetition of the song, together with the singer.

By the end of their second year more than 80 per cent of children can sing back something like what they have heard. About half of them at this age can produce something approximating to the words, rhythm and pitch of the model. Twelve per cent of the two year olds were even able to sing back whole songs – with mistakes.

A further 18 per cent were able to co-ordinate both the words and the rhythm, while the proportion of children who were able to co-ordinate the words only had dwindled to 4 per cent.

There was a separate group of 16 per cent of the two year olds, who did not sing words, but hummed or sang to the same syllable something similar to the rhythm and the pitch of the test, either while it was being played or after it had finished. Among the children of eighteen months this group was already as large as 12 per cent. Not one of the children aged eighteen months or of those aged two, in this group, sang the words of a song.

Some of the group of children who could co-ordinate words and rhythm did not always manage rhythm as well as words. Children who could sometimes keep to the words, rhythm and pitch of the test came out at other times with other songs which were all out of tune and rhythmically wrong. On the other hand, occasionally some of the children who usually only copied the words managed to sing something like the correct rhythm or even the right pitch.

To return to the 16 per cent who ignored the words: there were considerable variations in the degree of accuracy with which they imitated the rhythm and the pitch of the test, but they still never included a single word. So it is clear that there are two different ways in which a baby may set about imitating a sound that he has heard. This is surprising, and the reasons for it cannot be explained without further research.

The development of singing during the second year of life may be traced in broad outline through the songs in which words were sung. It begins with the words; then a little later children can match the rhythm of the model until, finally, they begin to approximate more closely to the pitch as well. At the same time the length of the piece of tune which the children are able to match, more or less correctly, extends from one or two notes or fragments of the words up to whole lines of a song, and with some children even to whole songs.

In the most successful attempts at imitating, the words are more or less correct, but there are some mistakes in the rhythm, while the least accurate is the pitch.

5. The Attitude of One to Two Year Olds to the Different Combinations of Words and Rhythm

In Test Series 2 the children were played one example each of 'Words with Rhythm', 'Rhythm with Words Added' and 'Nonsense-word Rhythm'. As was explained above, these three combinations of words and rhythm differed from the other tests in that no notes of fixed pitch were used. They differ from each other in that the relationship between music and speech is different in each one. Thus, in the first one, 'Words with Rhythm', the main purpose is that the words should make sense and the rhythmic pattern is only incidental, while in the second one, 'Rhythm with Words Added', the rhythmic pattern is more important than the meaning of the words. In the 'Nonsense-word Rhythm' syllables are simply put into a rhythmic pattern, and sounds which have no meaning were chosen deliberately. So the role of musical rhythm grows from the first to the third example, while that of communication through words decreases similarly. This test was planned to provide answers to the following two questions:

1. Do children respond in the same way to the different roles played by music and by speech?

2. What is the effect of the lack of notes of definite pitch?

The short answer is as follows: During the whole of their second year children respond in the same way to the roles played by music and by speech.

However, the children's responses to the tests did not give an absolutely clear answer, with all the subjects responding to the first test (Words with Rhythm) as if it were speech, and to the other two as if they were music. A 'simple answer' of this kind could not have been expected, since there is no such thing as a 'standard response' to the given tests. As was explained in the Introduction, the content of an experience is created in accord with the abilities and attitudes of the individual – during the process of experiencing. Since the aural stimulus in each test allowed for the possibility of a speech or a musical response; so in each particular case the form of the response may tend just as easily towards speech as towards music.[1]

So it is not at all remarkable for some of the subjects to respond to the same test with a musical response, while others react with a speech response. However, the response of each individual child ought to show an increase in musical response and a decrease in speech response from the first to the third test. This expectation was fulfilled with surprising clarity. Only three of the subjects responded to the first test as if it were music, and even in these three cases it was difficult to say whether or not this was a response to the piece of music which had just been played. What is quite certain, is that all the two year olds responded to the third test with a musical response. We were quite sure that one to two year old children can sort out the different roles played by music and speech, since they responded differently to the three tests. We classified as musical response: any attempt at singing, making repetitive movements, or vocalizations which indicated musical feeling; speech responses were, besides an attempt at talking, any actions or vocalizations which showed that the child understood some of the words. However varied the different responses were, they all showed an increase in the musical response and a decrease in the speech one from the first to the third test. So there is no doubt that one to two year olds are able to respond differently to the parts played by music and speech in the combinations of words and rhythm. 'Words with Rhythm' were far more often experienced as speech, while 'Nonsense-word Rhythms' were almost exclusively experienced as music. The middle test 'Rhythm with Words Added' was sometimes experienced as music, sometimes as speech. The proportion of two year olds who responded to this test as if it were speech was decidedly higher than it was with the younger children.

The second question to which this series was to provide an answer was: 'What effect does the lack of notes of fixed pitch have?'

1. H. G. Furth, in *Piaget and Knowledge*, 1969, p. 19, seems to express this idea more clearly. 'His [Piaget's] biological notion of an organism in constant interaction with its milieu is a rather commonplace notion, one would think; but this view has for Piaget the special implication that development and evolution are seen as intrinsic characteristics of the biological knowing process and not as events outside of the process. On the level of the theory of knowledge, this notion corresponds with the thesis that knowledge is neither solely in the subject, nor in a supposedly independent object, but is constructed by the subject as an indissociable subject–object relation.'

In seeking the answer to this question the response of the children to the third test was particularly interesting, since here were words, but meaningless ones. So what the children actually heard was nonsense vocal music without any definite pitch. Since the element of speech which is concerned with meaning was lacking completely, it is not surprising that from the two year olds (who have already reached the stage of being able to understand some of the function of speech as communication) all the responses were musical.

What is surprising however, is that this test, which did not contain any notes of fixed pitch, produced sung responses that were just as frequent as and no worse in quality than those sung to the well-known nursery songs.

The analysis of children's songs which was given in the last chapter showed that one to two year olds are more or less able to match their singing to a model, and that about half the children get as far as being able to copy differences of pitch. These tests showed how strong the musical effect is of the sound as a whole, and not just of the succession of sounds of different pitch. During the second year the child's powers of perception develop enough for him to begin to be able to sort out the different elements in the general sound and, since he is able to extend the range of his bodily movements, he begins to perceive what he hears as a sequence of events in time. Up to the age of a year the normal child is not capable of perceiving melodies as a succession of sounds of different pitch. Between the age of one and two he begins to be able to start arranging what he hears into a series of sounds. Thanks to his progress in intellectual development the child now begins to be able to sort out and put into order a series of sounds of different frequency, each of which only represents a fraction of the total sound. The tests proved, more conclusively than we had expected, that during the second year it is still sensory impression of the sound, together with the rhythm, which lie at the heart of musical experience.

4 · *The Musical Experience of the Child Between the Ages of Two and Three*

1. The General Development of the Child between the Ages of Two and Three

At this age the child shows increasing independence in all respects, though he still clings to his mother if he is tired or frightened.[1] All professional child-psychologists agree on the existence of this self-assertiveness, whether they label it as a separate stage of development, or consider it to be a transition between two stages. Changes in the internal structure of the personality do not necessarily take place; the self-assertiveness is much more likely to happen because the child has reached a stage of development in which he is capable of expressing himself as a person. It is this inner process of development rather than the outward manifestations of assertive behaviour which are of interest for us; for they influence the whole behaviour pattern of a child of this age, including his capacity for experiencing music. So the developmental changes which take place at this age will be outlined very briefly, and only in so far as they affect the ability to experience music.

This independence shows itself in tantrums if the child is frustrated. At this stage he is not yet aware of himself as something separate from his environment. People and things in his environment either seem to be part of himself, or they may be used as things to play with. The two year old cannot yet see them as objects in their own right; he is still in the process of discovering the boundary between himself and the surrounding world.

1. German authorities, e.g., Kroh, refer to this stage as 'the first period of defiance'. A. T. Jersild, *Child Psychology*, 1968, p. 221, 'In many children, resistance in relationships with their elders becomes most noticeable at about eighteen months and peaks at about the age of four. . . . This is the time when many children are acquiring and asserting what we call "a will of their own".'

So, in his fantasy world objects gradually cease to be thought of as behaving like people and are regarded in an objective way.

'He begins to differentiate between the various instinctive drives of his individual personality'. (Kroh 1944.) For example he defends his own possessions, he may show jealousy, or strive to be taken notice of as he tries to show his independence. There is a tendency towards self-protection and traits such as shyness, reserve and self-consciousness appear, together with their opposites, aggressiveness, envy and malice. An entirely new characteristic appears, since the child develops a 'will of his own'. He is restless and rebellious, and is not so easily distracted from his tantrums.

As these various developmental characteristics occur at the same time, some connection between them may be assumed. The common factor may be the beginnings of an awareness of the future. The will, according to Krudewig (1947, p. 24), is 'something which reaches forward into the future'; before a clear choice between two alternatives can be made 'it is necessary to possess the ability to foresee the consequences of two different courses of action' (Remplein 1964, p. 258). The ability to do this is one of the first signs of an awareness of the future. Awareness is also apparent in the case of his emotional needs and drives; for example the urge to possess something means to want to have it now and in the future; the urge to be taken notice of, too, does not apply only to the present but to the future as well; the urge to protect oneself is unthinkable unless there is more awareness of the future, and reserve can only be shown because one may be made to feel small if adults criticise or laugh *after* a child has done something wrong.

But *awareness* of the future is not the same thing as *happening* in the future. This awareness takes place through the mental present and, as the urge to give tit for tat clearly shows, according to what has happened in the past. This urge implies the desire to get even with someone in the future because of an insult suffered in the past; so the connection between the past and the future is clearly apparent. Indeed, if one thinks at all about the matter, obviously any concept of the future at all is only possible in the context of the past. Memory images, which make their first appearance at this stage of development, provide confirmation of this assumption, since in various different fields of experience the growing concept of past and future presupposes an extension of the mental present.

Since music can only exist in time, the extension of the mental present and the acquisition of memory must play an important part in musical experience. Awareness of past and future extends the child's ability to assimilate musical sounds in the way that one would expect, and, finally, the changes in the relationships between perception and feeling, and in those between the instinctual drives and feeling, also have an influence on musical experience.

2. Movements to Music

From about the age of two, children again begin to show a kind of behavioural response which is most unexpected in lively youngsters; it is concentrated, still, attentive listening. A child of this age has developed to the point of being able to forget himself and to give himself up to a musical experience. A remarkable number of children can sit as quiet as mice for as long as five minutes or more listening to music, paying no attention to other stimuli except when a particularly powerful aural stimulus, or an especially lively visual one, is presented to them. If, however, the children become aware of another aural or visual stimulus while they are listening, they not infrequently protest against the interruption. The attitude of many children of this age as they listen is so relaxed that they give an impression of meditating, and the observer may well be surprised to notice how children aged between two and three, who have only just become able to detach the self from its surroundings, are able, at the same time, to give themselves up to these surroundings at the very time that their developmental progress has made them able to achieve the necessary detachment.

The capacity of the two year old to lose himself in listening is quite different from the baby's earliest attentive listening, since his vocal and motor abilities are now developed and he is capable of responding to music by making sounds or movements; yet he sometimes deliberately chooses to listen quietly, though, as will be seen, he also responds by moving and by singing.

The type of behaviour just described accounts for the sharp drop in the number of movements observed in response to the tests. Moreover, now that the children are beginning to be able to concentrate for longer at a time they may be unwilling to leave off an activity once they have started on it. So, among other things, some of the music presented to the children may pass unnoticed, because their whole attention is actively engaged with something else. In administering the tests we tried to minimise this effect as much as possible by repeating a test if, when it was played to him the first time, the child was obviously absorbed in something else. So the drop in the number of motor responses ought to be caused principally by the change in the pattern of behaviour which has just been described.

Figure 6 shows the number of children of different ages who responded to music with repetitive movements. This number falls steeply from 36 to 27 at the age of two, and remains about the same throughout the third year. The number of movements observed among the children from one to two had already begun to fall, after rising steadily up to the age of one. The steepest drop is at the beginning of the third year, and this trend continues so clearly that only two-fifths of the number of movements shown by the one year olds were observed among the four year olds.

In contrast to the clear drop in the overall number of movements in response to the tests, the number of co-ordinated movements to music increases, especially during the third year. It would need a separate investigation to determine whether the comparatively small number of co-ordinated movements observed among the two year old subjects was a matter of chance, or whether it must be considered to indicate an aspect of development which has not yet been noted.

In the previous chapter we noticed how, in spite of the decrease in the number of movements to music which were observed there is an increase in the variety of movement. As Figure 6 shows, this trend continues up to the middle of the sixth year. The fractions in column five show the relation between the variety of movement for each child who responded by moving and the number of movements made by each subject.

Between the ages of two and three there is a slight decline in the variety of movement – caused by the decline in the overall number of movements; yet the relationship between the variety and number of rhythmic movements alters steadily in favour of variety of movement from between the ages of one and three, and this trend continues until the end of the pre-school period.

Co-ordinating movement with the rhythm of music which they hear clearly presents considerable difficulties for the children. Only one – a three year old girl – danced for a whole series of tests in time to the music. The other 20 children (9 aged two and a half and 11 aged three) among whom we observed any co-ordinated movements were only capable of keeping in time for a short stretch – anything from a few bars up to two or three lines of a song. Three records of the experiments show that even in these short stretches the children did not always keep absolutely in time, so that the extent of this ability is in fact still further limited.

At first children can keep time, not to music which they hear, but to their own spontaneous songs. In a few children this sort of co-ordination could be observed as early as the age of about eighteen months, but most children only manage to accompany part of their singing with rhythmically matching movements sometime between the ages of two and four. When they do this, children use movements which they have made in an unco-ordinated way to music which they have heard or sung themselves.

Only a few of the parents had watched this aspect of their children's behaviour carefully enough to be able either to report anything about the development of the child's ability to match his own singing and his move-ments; or to record the fact that he was able to achieve this co-ordination over a short space of time before he could manage to keep it up for longer.

One couple did report that some weeks went by between their first noticing co-ordination of this sort, and the next occasion on which they could be sure it had happened. However, even though this has not been carefully investigated, one may say, in the light of the research which has been done up till now, that children succeed in co-ordinating their move-ments with their own singing, for a short stretch at first and then gradually for longer at a time.

Figure 6. *Number and Variety of Motor Movements to Music*

Age of subject	Number of children who moved	Total number of movements observed	Number of subjects who could move in time with the music	Variety of movement of each subject who moved, in relation to the number of movements made by each subject
1.0	33	164	—	2.3:3.3
1.6	36	155	6	2.4:3.1
2.0	27	100	2	2.2:2.0
2.6	28	73	9	2.0:1.5
3.0	27	66	12	1.9:1.3
3.6	24	59	10	1.9:1.2
4.6	22	48	24	1.8:1.0
5.6	24	51	35	1.6:1.0

As was shown in the previous chapter, in order to be able to match the rhythm of his movements with the rhythm of sounds presented to him a child must be able to isolate the time element both of sounds and of movements before he can co-ordinate the one with the other. He is able to do this, not by a process of logical thought, but by adjusting his actions. However, this must present a real difficulty to him, as is shown by the small number of children who are able to do it and the short length of time that they are able to keep it up.

To a certain extent this difficulty is bypassed in the earliest instances we have mentioned, when children match their movements with their own singing. This singing is produced by motor actions of the vocal apparatus and the breath. The rhythm of these songs depends on the rhythm of the breathing, and the vocal apparatus joins in at the same speed, so that the singing and the motor movements of the vocal apparatus are dependent on the organs of breathing and must therefore be synchronized. Since the vocal organs and those concerned with breathing are synchronized in any case, co-ordinated movement in another part of the body may be considered as an extension of a co-ordinated movement which, in the case of the child's own singing, has already occurred between the vocal and breathing organs. So if it is a question of co-ordinating his movements with music which *he hears* and does not sing to, the child proceeds in the same way as if he were matching his singing to something which was sung to him. First he takes in the sound of the music. Children of this age do not make co-ordinated movements the first time they hear a piece. The number of repetitions needed for a child to be able to move in time to music which he hears depends on the individual ability of the child and also on the type of music played to him. In one case synchronized movements could be observed as early as the second repetition. Normally, rhythmically matched movements could only be observed after a number of repetitions, and to songs which were already known. The lullaby in Series 1 and the pop song in series 4 were accompanied particularly often with rhythmically correct movements, since both pieces were already well-known to most of the subjects.

A second group of children responded with rhythmically correct movements to the tests in which the rhythmic element predominated, i.e. the rhythm with added words, the nonsense word rhythms of Series 3 (Pure Rhythms) and the note-against-note cacophony in Series 5.

In these tests it is easier to master the difficulties which arise when the

rhythm of a series of sounds has to be transferred to a series of movements, since in these the attention of the children was concentrated on the
rhythm. In the two combinations of words and rhythm the absence of a
meaning in the words helps to ensure that the rhythmic impression is the
dominant one (Test Series 2.3); this may happen when the rhythm of the
sound does not follow the meaning of the words (Test Series 2.2), and the
lack of fixed pitch and harmony also serves to concentrate attention on the
rhythm. Thus any musical experience which goes beyond the mere
awareness of sounds can only take place in the rhythmic field, since this is
the one in which the source of musical stimulus lies.

The tests in Series 3 are even more clearly orientated towards rhythm,
since words, notes of fixed pitch, and harmony are completely lacking.
So the only possibility, beyond a simple awareness of sounds, is the
rhythmic one.

The situation is somewhat different with the deliberately distorted
harmonies of Series 5. The sounding of the keys of B major, B flat major,
C major, and D major simultaneously excludes any possibility of enjoying
the harmony, and at the same time this pile-up of dissonances destroys
the euphonious sound of each part on its own; so, as the melodies lose their
melodic significance in this way, there can be no question of clearly
appreciating the differences of pitch of the four melodies individually.
Only the rhythm remains intact, and thus becomes the dominant musical
element.

Even with these tests, in which the rhythmic element was especially
strong, the children did not at first move in time to the music. They began
by sitting still and listening for a while, before beginning to move in time
with the tests, and they were not able to co-ordinate their movements with
these tests, which were specially chosen for their rhythm, for longer at a
time than they were with the songs they already knew. Thus our experiments – though they were not specially designed for this purpose – showed
that neither songs which he knew already nor rhythmically strong music
had any significant effect on the child's ability to keep in time.

The movements made by children aged between two and three again
show an astonishing variety. The swaying backwards and forwards, the
rocking from side to side, and the jumping up and down appear frequently
at this age. Among the movements of parts of the body, 'conducting' and
swaying on one foot are the most common. Children are observed to clap

their hands more frequently, or to tap on a board on their knees, and also to move an object which they are holding.

Children aged between two and three make most spectacular progress in the way they use space as they move to music. A few little girls and boys made a circle round the room, and they moved in a way that really could be described as stepping.

By far the most frequent movements made by the three year olds were proper dance turns. The children would make a circle round the room, turning round as they went, and some of them swung a teddy or a doll or a soft toy most gracefully round with them. Four children danced themselves into a state of ecstasy by turning faster and faster in smaller and smaller circles.

Some strange combinations of movements occurred. One little girl combined swaying up and down by bending and stretching her knees with turning her shoulders from side to side, with her arms crossed in front of her chest. A small boy made a most artistic combination of movements, since he raised and lowered his shoulders swinging his arms round his body at the same time, first to one side and then to the other, also bending and stretching his knees, all in one continuous flexible movement.

A description can only give a pale shadow of the variety and charm of movement which three year old children make in response to music played or sung to them. The observer is, moreover, continually astonished at the feeling for space which children of this age develop, as they carry out these movements which are only partly in time with the music.

3. Songs

The same factor that produced a decline in the number of responses to music by rhythmical movements also leads, in the third year of life, to a fall in the number of responses in song. However, outside the test situation there is a marked increase in the amount of singing, both of songs resembling a model and of spontaneous ones which cannot be related to something learnt. During the third year of life children not only sing more often but also sing progressively longer snatches of either learnt or spontaneous songs.

a. *Spontaneous Songs*

In this group the increase in both number and length of songs is particularly noticeable, since there is no limit either to the length of individual lines or to that of the song as a whole. The child goes on singing spontaneously for as long as it amuses him. During the first half of the second year the spontaneous songs never lasted for more than a short while; between the ages of eighteen months and two years children begin to sing both more frequently and also for longer at a time, a trend which is continued and accelerated during the third year. Quite a number of children aged two and a half to three keep up spontaneous singing for over four minutes on end. Their songs are sometimes hummed to 'm' or 'ng' or sung on one vowel or one syllable. Now and again part of a word or even a whole one is included. Children of this age may also be heard singing spontaneously, using whole words most of the time, either repeating the same word over and over again or using a series of different ones. This use of words is a clear advance on the spontaneous singing of children aged one or two.

At first hearing, songs of this last type give the impression of narrative. But analysis of thirty-eight such spontaneous songs shows that the text sung hardly ever made any kind of sense. Five of the songs did however show some sort of meaning, so that it might have been assumed that the little singers expected the words of their songs to convey something to a listener. But in fact this was not so. The children simply sang to themselves, just like all those who sang nonsense songs. They were clearly pleased when one of the grown ups present told them how well they had sung, but none of them expected a reply from the adults there. Indeed, when at our request one mother did sing an answer, the baby was extremely surprised and stopped singing.

The rhythmic characteristic of spontaneous songs of children aged from eighteen months to two years, which we noticed in the previous chapter, can still be observed during the third year of life. A spontaneous song sung by a two or three year old is dominated by a single note-length, with varied groupings of notes into phrases giving the song some sort of structure. However, the total effect shows less variety than that of the songs of children aged about two; longer notes are not scattered about quite so freely. The rests between the individual phrases in the songs of three year olds are almost always short pauses for breath, and these follow more closely the overall pattern of the notes sung. In many spontaneous songs the underlying rhythmic pattern is duple. But children may add words which run counter to this underlying pattern (see Figure 7). During a song there are hardly ever any pauses of more than one beat; on the contrary the children much more frequently carry on singing in their simple rhythmic pattern for a long time without stopping. As in the second example given in Figure 7, the rhythmic pattern is sometimes still further emphasised by including from time to time two notes of the same pitch.

Figure 7. *Two spontaneous songs by a two year old child*

Irmgard F— (2 years 6 months)

b. *Songs which Imitate a Sung Model*

Between the ages of two and three all children of normal ability learn how to sing at least part of a song that has been sung to them. At the age of two only 80 per cent of the children we tested could do this.

This ability to learn, which had first emerged in the second year, continued to develop during the third, but of the two and a half year olds ten per cent were still able to imitate only the sound of the words, and of the three year olds there were four per cent who could still not recognizably imitate either the rhythm without the words or the pitch of the model.

Of the two and a half year olds 22 per cent could sing the words and also the rhythm, even when this was not reinforced by the speech-rhythm but could still not reproduce pitch correctly. By the age of three this percentage had dropped to ten, owing to the rapid increase in the size of the group of children who were able to reproduce pitch as well as words and rhythm. This last group increased only slowly during the first six months of the third year, comprising 40 per cent of the two year olds, 48 per cent of those aged two and a half, and then during the last six months of the second year suddenly rising to 80 per cent.

Of particular interest in this connection is the group of children who never imitated the words of the model. During the second year not one of these children altered his habit and sang the words of a song. We visited the subjects in this group several times and at last found two children who had previously never sung words beginning to imitate short snatches of the words of the sung model. One of these children was two and a half years old, the other was three. Statistical analysis of these tests and reports from parents confirmed that these could not be isolated cases. The rapid growth in size of the group of children who could imitate all three elements, words, rhythm and pitch, of a sung model occurs largely because children who had previously not sung the words begin at this age to include them. Thus the group of children who sang 'without the words' dwindles at this age from 16 to 6 per cent. The main reason for the increase in the number of children who sang the pitch in addition to the words and the rhythm is that those who had previously only sung words and rhythm now began to take notice of pitch as well.

Figure 8 (p. 98) gives a general survey of the development of imitative singing during the third year of life.

Most children begin, sometime between the ages of one and two, by imitating the words. Then a little later they begin to add the rhythm. Finally they reach the stage of imitating the pitch as well. During the second half of the third year each of the children at the stages we have just described progressed, on average, one stage further. The four per cent who had previously not been able to imitate at all were now, at the end of their third year, in the category of 'word singers'; the ten per cent of two-and-a-half-year-old 'word singers' now appeared as 'word and rhythm singers' while the 22 per cent of the two-and-a-half-year-old 'word and rhythm singers' were now included in the 80 per cent of the three year old subjects who could imitate pitch as well as words and rhythm.

The number of children who could now manage whole songs also increases most noticeably. In the course of one year the proportion of these rises from an eighth to just about half the children. If one can justifiably say that by the end of the second year all children can more or less sing, then it may equally well be said that by the end of the third year all children are capable of imitative singing.

About half of the three year olds could sing the words, rhythm and pitch of a whole song more or less correctly (see transcription in Figure 9). Like the one to two year olds, the children aged two to three are most successful at imitating the sound of the words; they make more mistakes in the rhythm, especially if this does not follow the word pattern; and the

Fig. 9 Two 'similar' songs of three-year old children

Bärbel W— (3 years 6 months) 'Come lovely May'

—lie – ber Mai   und ma – – che   die Bäu – me

wie – – der   grün   und lass   mer an   den

Ba – – che   die klei – nen   Veil – chen glüh'n. . .

Dirk P— (2 years 6 months) 'Hänsel and Gretel'

Dirk :

Hän – sel und Gre – tel   ich – ten sich

Mother :

Hän – sel und Gre – tel ver –

im Wald.   dun – tel   auch   bit –

im Wald.   Es   war so

– te tal.   ta – ben an   am Häus – – chen

Sie

98

greatest difficulties continue to be presented by differences of pitch. In this case the word 'imitate' simply means that the direction of the melody is followed. 'Micromelodies' may still be heard during the third year, though less frequently than before. But the 'imitation', so far as pitch is concerned, often simply means that only some groups of notes are sung correctly. When children sing with the tests, their singing may often be heard as a parallel melody. During this year all the various types of inability to imitate are much less in evidence, and the groups classed as 'able to imitate' include a number of children who are not far off being able to sing absolutely correctly. However, only two per cent of our subjects aged between two and three were able to sing a whole verse of a song without making any mistakes at all.

Among the children aged two to three there is another type of singing,

Figure 8. *The Development of Imitative Singing between the Ages of Two and Three*

Years	2.0	2.6	3.0
Songs with no resemblance to model	20%	4%	0%
Songs which resemble the sound of the words	18%	10%	4%
Songs which resemble the words and the rhythm	6%	22%	10%
Songs which resemble the words, rhythm and pitch for part of a song	28% ⎫	26% ⎫	36% ⎫
Songs which resemble the words, rhythm and pitch for a whole song	12% ⎭ 40%	22% ⎭ 48%	44% ⎭ 80% (2% of these sing without mistakes)
Songs which resemble rhythm and pitch	16%	16%	6%

which is difficult to classify as either 'imitative' or spontaneous. With younger children one hears either spontaneous singing which bears no relationship to known songs, or singing which shows that the child is trying, with varying degrees of success, to imitate something that has been sung to him. However, in this third, mixed form the child begins to sing spontaneously but lets fragments of the words or melodies of songs he has learnt come into his singing as he goes along. So bits of the words of a learnt song may be mixed with an 'original melody'. This must not be put down to inability to imitate: it is simply that the child feels like putting into his own songs bits of the tunes he has learnt – making up his own words for them. He is not in the least concerned with singing songs he knows already but is including his existing musical experience in his vocal improvisation. We will call this type of singing 'pot-pourri' songs.

With the younger children we gave up the attempt to determine the precise range of their voices and simply gave one or two indications of its extent. But with children aged two to three, in view of the greater length of their songs, it seems reasonable to try to say what vocal range they used.

In this investigation particular weight was given to the spontaneous songs, since here the little singer can himself decide how high or low he sings.

The lowest note we heard from among the three year olds was a♭; the highest was g″. In both cases we were able to prove that the child had adopted the vocal range of his mother.

A quarter of the children used a range of one-and-a-half octaves, with half the children the range was between one and one-and-a-half octaves, and only the remaining quarter used a range of less than an octave. The smallest range used was a fifth, the largest a twelfth. The average range was a little over an octave. The average middle note of the children's songs was f♯′. So the average range of the two to three year olds we tested was more or less the first octave in the treble clef.

A similar investigation was carried out by Werner in 1917. The average vocal range of the two to three year olds we observed is wider than that given by Werner, which he established with the help of records, using children up to the age of five as subjects. The average middle note of his two to three year olds is lower than the one we found: his was around d♭′. The result of both pieces of research was surprising, since vocal training today begins from a much higher range of pitch (Kemper 1951; Nitsche 1952).

4. Music and Speech

We know from the analysis of children's singing that two to three year olds are still better at reproducing the words than they are at copying the rhythm and the pitch – which goes on presenting the greatest difficulties. But the fact that the words have meaning is not what makes them easier for the children to grasp; children copy them first when learning to sing because their sound makes the strongest impression.

In the previous chapter the response of two year olds to the tests in Series 2 (Different Combinations of Words and Rhythm) was discussed, together with the question whether children responded differently to the roles played by music and by speech. We considered the same question in relation to the two to three year old subjects and were able to say with certainty that, at this age too, the individual responses of each child differed according to the importance of the role played by the musical element in the test. Whenever a child responded to more than one item in Series 2 (Combinations of Words and Rhythm) his responses always showed an increase in musical response and a corresponding decline in speech response. A few children who *talked* during Tests 1 or 2, *sang* during Test 3. Their spontaneous comments referred to Test 1 as 'talking', while they called the second or the third test 'singing'. Rocking or swaying movements were larger and stronger to the later ones than to the first test of Series 2. These are just a few examples of the many responses which showed that children in their third year still reacted differently to the distinctive roles of music and speech in the combinations of words and rhythm. Some of the children's remarks showed how clearly they were able to make this distinction, as when a small boy said: 'They are saying a song' when Test 2 was played, or when another small boy replied to the question 'What is that?' when the same test was played, by beginning to repeat a short rhyme. However, such fine distinctions were not made very often.

Taking the responses of the children to Series 2 as a whole, it is surprising to find that the combination of words and rhythm in Test 3, which is meaningless nonsense, produced about a third more responses than the combinations of words and rhythm in Tests 1 and 2, which did make sense. The number of reactions to Test 1, where the sense of the words is the most important element, was the lowest. In Test 2 the sense of the words is less important than the rhythmic pattern, since a 'foreign' rhythm is imposed on them. This increase in the importance of the rhythm and the corresponding decline in the importance of the sense of the words produced about seven per cent more responses than the first test.

How much the sound of the rhythm, rather than the content of the meaning, is the dominant impression with children of this age is shown by another result from this series of tests. Adults always react to the combinations of words and rhythm in Tests 1 and 2 as if these were speech. A mature person considers the rhythmic pattern of the words as something incidental, while their meaning is, for him, the most important thing. Adults even feel that the string of nonsense syllables in Test 3 ought to have some meaning, and this test seems to them to be musically lacking in something.

Half of the two to three year old children reacted to the first two tests, which for us are definitely speech, as if they were music. They react to these as if the tests were music more than younger children do.

The rhythmic pattern in Test 1 was enough for many children to give them the idea that this test was music. When the rhythm became still more important, in Test 2, the number of children who reacted musically rose by ten per cent (see Figure 10). The nonsense-word rhythm of Test 3 was one of the tests which the children liked best in the whole series. Not a single child complained that the words had no meaning.

The results of the tests support the observations of many parents, who know that two or three year olds listen most attentively to poems and rhymes.

In Test Series 3 children heard rhythms without any words. The absence of words has an astonishing effect. Thirty-seven per cent of the children simply ignored the test, even when the volume was considerably increased. Twenty-four per cent of the subjects showed signs of being uneasy, and linked the sounds which they heard with things outside the realm of music that made noises. One little boy asked his mother, when this test was played, 'When are we going to have music again?' and another said, 'That isn't music, is it Mummy?'

This indirect question is characteristic of the uncertain response of a third group of 14 per cent of the subjects, who sometimes responded with babbling songs or movements as if they were hearing music but at other times connected these tests with things which made noises.

Figure 10. *Number and type of response to Test Series 2*

	Test 1: 'Words with Rhythm' (spoken meaningfully take on a rhythmic pattern)		Test 2: 'Rhythm with Words Added' (words put into a rhythmic pattern which does not fit pattern of words if these are spoken meaningfully)		Test 3: 'Nonsense-word Rhythm' (string of syllables arranged in a rhythmic pattern)	
	Speech Response	Music Response	Speech Response	Music Response	Speech Response	Music Response
Number	23	20	20	26	—	60
Percentage	53%	47%	43%	57%	0%	100%
Number	43		46		60	
Percentage of total responses	29%		31%		40%	

Only 14 per cent of the children felt that the test series of pure rhythms was music, without any reservations at all.

These reactions to Series 3 guard against a possible misinterpretation of the responses to the combinations of words and rhythm. These could be interpreted in the following way: it was the rhythmic pattern alone which particularly attracted the children's attention, so that if the words were not there, and a similarly arresting rhythm was played, then the children would take notice of the rhythm. But the behaviour of the children when they heard the rhythms without words excludes this possible interpretation. It is not just the rhythmic pattern, but the combination of this with the sound of the words, that attracts two to three year olds so strongly. If the sound is poorer, then the children lose interest in what is played to them (A. Nestele 1930; F. Brehmer 1925).

The adult cannot easily get over his habit of listening for a meaning when he hears speech, and give himself up completely to the sound of the words. But a conscious effort should be made, once, to adopt this unusual attitude towards speech if one is to understand how right a child is to enjoy this wealth of sound.

So the overall sound of the words is still a most important element in the child's experience of music. He is clearly now able to take in something which extends over a period of time, and should therefore be able to take in melodies as well. But the child experiences melodies, less as a series of rhythms and pitches, more as modifications of the general sound that is going on in which the speech sound is of prime importance. Not one child asked for sounds of fixed pitch, either during the playing of the combinations of words and rhythm or of those with pure rhythm; and from the children's singing we know that exact pitch still presents considerable difficulties. These difficulties become understandable if one realises that the child is still bound to the general impression of the sound as a whole, in which pitch represents a relatively abstract element.

The strong impression which the sound of the words still makes on the child, and that of the sense impression of the sound generally, is apparent in his ability, or lack of it, to recognize music when it is played again. Only ten per cent of the children recognized songs when these were played on an instrument, while, in contrast, eleven per cent were already able to recognize an instrument by its tone colour. This low percentage can only be seen in its true perspective when one considers how few children of this age have an opportunity to hear different instruments at all. A number of three year olds showed an ability similar to the recognition of instruments when, on hearing a piece of music played in one of the tests, they recalled a situation in which they had heard the same music before. Both these instances of ability to remember rest on a single overall sense impression, and are much easier for a child than the recalling of a song when the speech sound of the words is lacking, and when this element, so important for a child, is replaced by a different sound: that of an instrument.

Four children showed a most strange mixture of speech and musical response to music. They stood out from the others because they learned to sing long before they learnt to talk. Between the age of a year and eighteen months they were already singing surprisingly long snatches of songs, and by the age of eighteen months they were able to sing whole verses or pieces of music, always, of course, either humming or singing on one syllable. The chief representative of this group sang the theme from Haydn's *Drum Roll Symphony* as his very first song and by the age of two he had a 'repertoire' of more than twenty songs.

The really strange thing about this small group of singers is not, however, the fact that they learnt to sing long before they learnt to talk. Even more strange seems to be the way in which these children feel that differences of pitch and rhythm mean different things, just like different words in speech.

In one case the exchange of the roles of speech and music was a pathological condition. (The little girl was four when she was introduced to us.) The speech centre of her brain had been damaged by illness, and the ability to imitate rhythms had taken the place of the ability to reproduce speech sounds. When a short remark was made to the child she could only hum the rhythm back, but with this 'morse code' she was able to keep up some sort of speech contact with her family, however weak this contact was. The three other little 'talking singers' – who were all boys – sang, to 'oo', 'ho', 'ng', or 'm', series of sounds which had a definite meaning. For instance, one of them always greeted one of the grown ups whom he knew by singing the song which that person had taught him; another boy sang snatches of songs to 'm' and clearly connected them with the meaning of words which he could neither say nor sing, and he attached particular meanings to particular bits of melodies. The tune of a modern dance meant something like 'Come and dance with me', a fragment of another song told anyone who was near him that he would like some water to water the flowers with, an occupation in which he was often engaged. The third little singer also had a number of bits of music which all meant something, like a short, partly-gurgled song, which was always the same and which meant 'I'm thirsty'. The beginning of a lullaby replaced the well-known German baby word *Heia* and was used when he was rocking a woolly animal as well as an accompaniment to a signal that he did not want to go to bed. We were able to observe two of these children's progress for over a year. Both learnt to talk very quickly about the age of three and they are clearly exceptionally gifted.

5 · The Musical Experience of the Child aged from Three to Four

1. General Development between the Age of Three and Four Years

Sometime between the age of three and three and a half the child's general behaviour becomes more amenable; the pendulum swings back and he becomes less aggressive. He has succeeded in separating what he perceives from what is within himself, so his perception is now objective; it no longer has such a strong link with his emotions as during the previous years, when he was unable to distinguish between his fantasy world and the world of objective reality. As he becomes more aware of things as something apart from himself the emotional element in perception becomes less important, the intellect plays a greater part, and perception is more and more influenced by previous experiences. Thought is still tied to things in immediate experience, and continues to be closely connected with concrete objects or events (Piaget 1948). Individual children vary considerably in the extent to which their perceptions are still influenced by their emotions; they are still clearly influenced by what they see and hear. In spite of all his questions about why, the child does not yet possess the insight into causality to explain everything he perceives, so it is the emotions aroused by his perceptions which are most apparent; but, since his power of logical thought has developed considerably, true make-believe people and objects replace the earlier undifferentiated vague general impressions. These make-believe people are the product of a free and lively fantasy, but even though the imaginative explanation of them is utterly unreliable they must still be regarded as an attempt to master and explain the significance of the world of reality. This 'magical attitude' as Kroh (1944) calls it, which is characteristic of the three year old, is thus part of the process of the child's development of a more objective view of the world around him.[1]

Kroh mentions another important sign of progress between the ages of three and four; the child is now able to conform to accepted social behaviour, in that he is able to play with other children, show affection for younger brothers and sisters, and understand sharing toys. He likes to be with other people; earlier his relationship with others was simply an acceptance that an adult looked after him, but now his social behaviour shows that he wants to act in common with other people. However, his play is often a 'parallel-play' rather than a true playing together with other children. Several children simply play at the same game alongside each other and imitate each other (Busemann 1953). But there are also clear signs of concern for others (Lersch 1962).

The child's greater awareness of reality and his progress in social development make him much easier to manage at home, and he is also ready to join with other children in a nursery school, although the age at which this occurs varies according to the child's type of personality and his individual make-up.[2]

At this age children give themselves up wholeheartedly to all forms of play, either on their own, or imitating each other in 'parallel play' or in genuine social playing together.

2. Movements to Music

In the previous chapter, when we were discussing the behaviour of children aged between two and three, we mentioned that many of them when listening to music simply sat still and concentrated. This sort of listening behaviour, where the child makes no outward responses either in movement or in attempts at singing became much more common after the third birthday. When the tests were given to the three year old subjects, ten per cent of them, throughout the whole series, simply sat still

---

1. A. T. Jersild, *Child Psychology*, 1968, p. 386, 'Make believe is impelled by all the motives that underlie human activity. In his earliest imaginative activities, a child uses make believe as a form of play in connection with his own self-initiated impulse to use his growing powers. Make believe also serves as a means of dealing with problems'.

2. Remplein (1964) has called the age from three and a half to five and a half 'the age of serious play'.

and concentrated. Meanwhile their breathing became slower and shallower, until, at the end of a piece they gave a deep sigh – an indication of their first deep breath since the music began.

As was expected, during the fourth year the total number of movements to music declined still further. Of the subjects aged three and a half only 25 showed such responses. Movements actually in time with the music were made by 10 of the children. The total number of movements observed in response to the tests dropped to 57, as opposed to 666 among the three year olds (see Figure 6, p. 91). If we consider together the total number of movements observed and the number of children who made such responses the percentage of children who moved actually in time to the music is seen to remain more or less constant.

But contrary to what might be expected, we could find no further increase in the number of instances of co-ordination between movement and music. On the other hand, the relative *variety* of movements increased again, from 1.9:1.3 to 1.9:1.2. In counting up the different movements, if more than one was made at the same time they were treated as separate movements. For example, a little girl danced with her arms outstretched and swung them up and down, and a small boy rocked his head and swung his foot at the same time.

However, the full variety cannot be grasped simply by considering the various movements which were made at the same time, since many of the motor movements were themselves a combination of several ones made simultaneously. In the children's dancing it was possible to distinguish stepping from running or turning, but how far little movements such as curtseys, head nodding, arm swinging and the like were to be considered as separate movements rather than as part of the main movement was seldom clear. In counting up these movements, only those which seemed to be made relatively independently of each other were classed as separate.

Several of the simultaneous movements occurred mainly during dancing. The children usually danced on their own; only a quarter provided themselves with a partner, by asking a parent or brother or sister to dance with them, or, as some children did, by making a partner of a teddy or some sort of doll or soft toy like children a year younger (see Chapter 4).

It would be rash to assume from this that at this age only about 25 per cent of children were able to show social behaviour in their movements to music, when their social relationships in other fields of experience were much more developed.

A far greater proportion of children would have liked a partner in their dancing. This was obvious from the large number who asked some of the grown ups present to join in with their round games, but whose requests were refused. Other children also must certainly have experienced this sort of negative response, adapted their behaviour to it, and given up asking adults to join in with them.

There are further points about social relationships which should be taken into account. It is the person who accepts an invitation to join in with some sort of social activity, as well as the one who takes the initiative in making contact with others, who shows a wish for a social relationship. So truly anti-social behaviour should be attributed only to the person who makes no response at all to a request to join in social activity.

Although three quarters of the three to four year old children did not take the social initiative of asking someone to dance with them, none of them refused the invitation to join in a round game if it was offered.

We carried out further tests and asked parents or brothers and sisters of the subjects to play a round game with the toddlers when Series 1 was played. The children, without exception, happily accepted the invitation; so these further experiments confirmed our view that so far as music is concerned social behaviour is not restricted to those children who take the initiative in demanding it.

Only a minority took the initiative themselves; three quarters of the children needed to be invited.

Later the parents of the children with whom we had carried out these further experiments reported that their children, having played a round game once, often asked to play one again; so it may fairly be assumed that children must first experience social dancing before they themselves can show a wish to do it. Thus the general tendency of children of this age towards communal activity appears in relation to music, as in other aspects of life, and as one would expect, these children, who enjoy social contacts generally, could easily be brought to join in a communal dance – even though they were not in the category who spontaneously sought out a partner.

One other result of these further experiments must be expressed in the form of a question, to which an answer could only be provided by further research. Surprisingly enough, there were a number of children who, according to their parents, could only with difficulty be persuaded to join in a game with other people but who were ready without much hesitation to join in a round dance. It would be of practical educational interest to undertake an empirical investigation into the question of how far children who have difficulty in making contact with others would willingly join in when moving to music, though otherwise preferring to remain on their own.

As was stated above, long before the age of two some children begin to show a wish to dance with an adult when music is played. Then the movements made are not communal in the sense that *both* participants follow some sort of order or sequence in their movements. The reason why movements are matched to each other is that the grown-up adapts his movements to those of the child. It is often simply a question of completely different actions being made by two people at the same time.

After the age of two and a half the child begins to join in, himself. The actions of the grown up may still be quite different from those of the child, but the toddler no longer simply lets the movements happen; he makes some attempt to control them. So one may see that awareness of reality has extended into the realm of music. The child acts in company with someone else, according to the demands of the music played and also in response to the person he is dancing with.

The ability of the three to four year old to adjust his movements to what he hears and to his social surroundings, even though most children are unable to keep in time with music, shows clearly how strongly social behaviour is integrated with general development. The child's growing ability to order his behaviour in accordance with what is happening around him shows itself in the most varied spheres of activity. In social relationships it appears as an ability to adapt to people; in relation to objects it appears as a more detailed awareness of reality than before; in the field of speech, it shows itself as markedly rapid progress in vocabulary and in use of language; and, among its many other manifestations in other fields, this growing ability to co-ordinate appears also in relation to music.

As was stated previously, true, exact co-ordination of movement and music is achieved by only one child in ten. However, most children can by this stage make the broad distinction between fast and slow. Half a dozen of the small subjects made up genuine expressive dances [*Ausdruckstanze*] to the music they heard, and of these children two little girls danced with a kind of ecstasy. Though they did not keep exactly in time with the music the children made the most varied curving shapes about the room as they turned, stepped, or ran. For the first time we noticed that the children changed direction as they danced. Now and again the young dancers paused, staying on the same spot with arms raised, or crouching down, rocking backwards and forwards, or rising up on to the tips of the toes and then down again, as they responded in movement to the sounds they heard. Several children also stopped moving, and listened motionless to the music for a while, before continuing their dancing.

These astonishingly complex dances were in sharp contrast to the simple series of indiscriminate rocking movements, whose only relationship to the music heard was often, merely that movement and music took place at the same time.

Nevertheless, between the ages of three and four, simple jumping and rocking movements, such as those made by much younger children, may still be observed twice as frequently as proper dance movements. Many children who dance make these simple rocking movements as well. From the age of three onwards movements of individual parts of the body become increasingly frequent, and are met with almost as often as rocking movements. The following movements of parts of the body were observed among the three year old subjects:

1. Rocking feet
2. Moving the mouth rhythmically
3. Nodding the head
4. Rocking the head from side to side
5. Circling outstretched arms
6. Swinging outstretched arms
7. Drum beating
8. Hand clapping.

These movements have been listed in order of frequency, beginning with the most frequent. It is noticeable how rarely the children clapped to music, all the more so in that clapping is so widely used in the musical education of older children.

Between the ages of three and four another stage in the development of movement and music can be clearly distinguished. Previously the child carried out his movements – highly varied, even though always some kind of swaying – without any further purpose. The motor movements were simply the translation into movement of what he heard. Thus the games which adults played with children aged between one and two were merely sequences of definite, simple movements to particular songs. The movement was made simply for its own sake. But between the ages of two and three movement *to* music as well as movement *with* music slip unnoticed into children's play. Children may pick something up, in order to move it as they listen. The social urge also appears, as we have described, and the children become increasingly interested in types of music, as well as in games involving both music and movement. At this stage the child enjoys singing and moving as he plays. The successful translation into action of this new attitude to music cannot be clearly seen until some time after the age of three; before that age children can do too little for any change to be apparent.

But this stage of development is not as clearly marked as one could wish, owing to a further circumstance. Until the age of about three the development of a response to music was determined by innate ability and by the musical stimuli presented to the child more or less haphazardly. At its earliest stage the development of musical potential depended only to a small extent on the provision of chosen stimuli, to which the child more or less had to respond. Far and away the most important factor in determining the difference in response was the difference in musical or general ability. But now, given a particular level of ability, a child needs more than some chance musical stimulus to help him make forms of movement other than the instinctive swaying one. To make these new movements a child has to learn singing games and round dances. Up till the age of about three we could not observe in response to music any significant differences determined by the environment; children from poorer homes reacted no differently to our tests from children from the upper income groups. Children who, according to their parents' reports, were inundated with music from morning till night showed little difference, in either the quantity or quality of their response, from children who were only allowed to hear carefully weighed amounts of carefully chosen musical stimuli. This discovery was quite the reverse of what we had expected to find when starting the experiments.

But, between the ages of three and four, differences in home environment begin to show their effect in the field of music. Girls and boys who are taught songs and games by their parents brothers and sisters, or in nursery schools, have a clear advantage over other children. But the number of parents who teach their children songs and games is scandalously low.

Most mothers do not know any singing games suitable for this age. The chief source of songs and games is the nursery schools, which have the indirect effect of teaching the parents since the children bring their songs and games home.

Owing to the influence of the environment the true stage of musical development at the age of four may be best described by showing what is possible for a child of this age, rather than what he actually does. If he is taught in a way suitable for his age a four year old is quite capable of learning singing games and dances, a clear advance over the various kinds of swaying movements and instinctive dancing that constituted his previous repertoire.

3. Songs

During the fourth year, as one would expect, the number and scope of children's songs continues to increase. The number of songs observed during the tests did, indeed, fall and we will discuss this in the next section of the chapter. But we observed songs mainly during the preliminary discussion before the tests were given, and before or after the tests. The work with children of this age was made much easier by their comparative readiness to sing, and because they sing a great deal anyway; so it was easy to record on tape an example of most of these children's singing.

One of the three to four year old subjects had, according to his parents, not yet sung and he did not make a single sound in response to the tests. The whole behaviour of this boy seemed to show that he was severely retarded; so from the point of view of the development of singing his case cannot be considered at all normal. It is mentioned here simply because, of all the subjects over two years old, he was the only one who had not yet sung.

a. *Spontaneous and Imaginative Songs*

In addition to the 'spontaneous songs' and the 'imitative songs' of three to four year olds there emerges a third group, 'imaginative songs'. This group consists partly of spontaneous singing by the children, partly of snatches of songs which they know or new versions of these. Only twelve of the forty-nine three year old subjects of normal development (about

25 per cent) sang spontaneous songs with no resemblance to a known song. Sometimes this singing was just humming, or singing to one syllable, when a radio or a record was played. Other children sang away to themselves while they were playing, repeating a short verbal phrase or even a single word, over and over again.

For instance a boy sat on the floor in the kitchen playing with saucepan lids and spoons, and singing continuously 'Pomme, Hotta', which his mother interpreted as '*Komm, Pferdchen!*' [Come little pony!]. In this song, which had an 'ostinato text', the rhythm hardly varied at all. Most variations of rhythm were determined by the repetition of the first or the second word. The melodic line was repeated several times without alteration, then again a few more times with variations, using a range of more than one and a half octaves. Like this little boy, a little girl of the same age kept on singing the name of her hedgehog toy (*Mecki*) as she dressed it.

During the fourth year there was a great extension of the 'pot-pourri' songs which we had at first noticed among a fairly small group of two and a half to three year olds. In these songs children make up new ones by putting together pieces of several songs which they already know. Words, melodic lines and rhythms are mixed up, altered, taken apart and put together again in a different way and then fitted-in between stretches of 'original ideas'. (See transcription, Figure 11, p. 116.)

Narrative songs show a similar development to the 'pot-pourri' songs, though with four year olds they still hardly deserve this name. Any words are sung so long as they seem to tell a story, but the child sings without trying to tell the story to another person, carrying on as if he were quite alone. These sung monologues are interspersed with nonsense interpolations if the little singer cannot think of suitable words which make sense. Occasionally, little pieces of learnt songs find their way into the narrative songs.

The astonishing variety in the spontaneous singing is partly a sign of lively intellectual activity; but on the other hand the imagination needs something to work on, and the use of snatches of learnt songs shows how the necessary material is provided; the child rearranges and finds new ways of expressing what he has already taken in.

Over 30 per cent of the three to four year old subjects sang 'pot-pourri' songs. Some of these were the same children as those who sang narrative songs – that did not resemble songs which they knew. More than half the three to four year olds observed sang some sort of original song, either related to a song they already knew, or bearing no resemblance at all to anything learnt.

In a few isolated cases the imagination of the children was far enough developed to go beyond the mere rearrangement of what they had already

Fig. 11   Original Songs of Three to Four-year Olds

'Pot-pourri' song

Rhythmic variation

heard; figures or phrases from a learnt song were altered according to a definite formal principle. The achievement of three and a half year old B— was extraordinary from this point of view; she sang the whole of the Christmas carol '*Ihr Kinderlein kommet*' [Come little children] with the time altered from four to three. B— could, according to her father, sing the song just as well in the right metre (see transcription, Figure 11). Even a wrong note at the end of the right version of the song must be to the credit of the little girl, since after singing a wrong note only the most gifted children could, according to our observations, return to the right key.

There are so many of these original songs and they are always sung so attractively and often sound so charming that, in evaluating them, it is easy to overlook a major defect: they are very poor in rhythmic invention. Duple time predominates, as with two to three year olds – and usually notes of only two different lengths are used. Now and again spontaneous songs using only notes of the same length could be heard. If a note of a third or fourth length is included this is always due to the rhythm of the words. But even in the simple rhythm in duple time which the children use, the words play an important part. Now and again a simple rhythmic scheme may be maintained, once it has been started, against the rhythm of the words. The most striking example of this is the Christmas carol which three and a half year old B— sang in three time, as we described just now. A glance at children's songbooks shows how our nursery songs reflect the rhythmic simplicity of children's original songs (J. Wenz 1949; F. Jöde n.d.). Nursery teachers know well how the few dotted rhythms that there are get 'ironed out' by the children, while two notes slurred to one syllable present no difficulty at all.

b. *Learnt Songs*

Only two among the three to four year old subjects still kept to the words alone in their efforts to imitate a song. These two children could not imitate the rhythm when it departed from that of the words, and they had not the slightest idea of how to get anywhere near the pitch of the songs which were sung to them.

Only one child in this age group still sang snatches of songs *without words* but with the correct rhythm and pitch; this child sang a parallel melody to that of the model, but with all the intervals made smaller. Since we know that this habit of singing smaller intervals is a way of singing which reaches its 'peak' with younger children this child was probably a late developer from that group of subjects (16 per cent) which began its imitative singing with matching the rhythm and pitch of the model, and did not sing the words (see Chapter 3).

These children begin to include words sometime between the age of two and three. The singing of the three to four year old subjects showed finally that, with this exception, the children who had begun by not imitating the words could all do so by the time they had reached this age. So they are no longer distinguishable from the much larger group of children, who began their attempts at imitative singing by copying the words.

The process of development may be summarized as follows:

Figure 12. *Imitative songs of three to four year old children*

1	2	3	4	5
Words only similar or correct	Words and rhythm similar or correct	Words, rhythm and pitch similar or with up to one line correct	Whole songs correct (apart from some small errors)	Rhythm and pitch only more or less correct
4%	18%	38%	38%	2%

76% of four year olds
sing more or less correctly

Eighty-four per cent of subjects begin to imitate a model sung to them, some time between the age of one and two by imitating the words. They only begin to try to match the pitch of a model when they can copy both the words and the rhythm in a recognizable way.

Sixteen per cent of the subjects begin to imitate a model sung to them, some time between the age of one and two by copying the rhythm and pitch of the song without the words.

The second group – with the one exception – learns to copy the words as well some time during the third year of life. So the proportion of subjects who could sing words rhythm and pitch, or even whole songs, more or less correctly, rises abruptly between the ages of two and four. Children who begin to imitate by not copying the words can sing more or less correctly by the age of three and a half. In Figure 12 they are included in columns three and four. The subjects referred to in columns one and five are exceptions.

Children who sang 'words only' and children who sang 'without words' must show about the same degree of backwardness.

The 18 per cent of the three to four year old subjects, in column two, who still did not try to imitate the pitch, must have begun by imitating the words.

Of the 84 per cent who began imitative singing by copying the words, more than one child in five is still not able to manage pitch by the end of the fourth year. But every child in the group that began by imitating rhythm and pitch can, if his development is normal, manage the words as well by the same age.

These results lead to the following conclusions: Children who begin to imitate without singing the words learn to sing more or less correctly between the age of three and four. About a fifth of the children who began by imitating the words still cannot manage pitch by the end of their fourth year. It would be interesting to investigate whether these two groups show significant differences in other fields of learning, or in experience other than in the growth of intellectual ability.

From the age of two onwards the development of imitative singing depends more on the child's musical environment than it did at an earlier age. A large number of the children who could sing parts of songs correctly would surely have managed a whole song if they had been given sufficient encouragement to do so. A number of four year olds had already got a 'repertoire' of five to ten or more songs. They would never have had this if they had not been taught the songs.

The nursery schools play a most important part in teaching children songs: many children owe their store of songs entirely to the nursery school – but many mothers would like to sing to their children if they themselves knew suitable songs.

The children who had the largest repertoire of all came, according to our observations, without exception from homes where the parents sang particularly often. However, sometimes parents or grandparents went too far in this direction and were over ambitious for the children.

There is a connection between the songs which are learnt and the original songs, as children who have learnt a few songs go on to sing original songs using the same forms. On the other hand we had great difficulty in getting an example on tape of an original song of any sort from the children who still could not sing a learnt song. It was not possible to establish in detail the extent to which the approach to music is determined by the relative amount of original singing and of imitative singing, nor how far the original singing was helped through the learning of songs.

4. Play and Music

Children's play shows clear parallels with imaginative singing. Toys, and things which are used as toys, are arranged and rearranged in the greatest possible variety of ways; this is especially true when the toy is not something which can only be used for one purpose, but which offers all sorts of different possibilities. The child explores 'what goes with what' and so, within the limits of his ability and his attention span, he finds out by using them the properties of things which are given to him.

When he uses his imagination musically there is an added advantage: the range of musical imagination is not limited by objective reality. Figures, rhythms and sounds can be arranged in any conceivable order, in ugly or nonsensical sequences. Even though ugly sounds may not conform to the laws of aesthetics, aesthetics cannot prevent their existence; so, paradoxically, the ugly is possible in the realm of aesthetics.

In the world of objective reality the scope for imagination is distinctly narrower. The nature of the material itself limits the possibilities of its uses, and each time something is completed the possibilities of use are limited still further. Music enjoys a particularly high degree of freedom, in that it is not determined by objective reality. However, this very ease with which musical imagination can range imposes certain demands, forcing the creative musician to come to some decision amidst the infinite number of sounds which might be, and to consider what function a sound is to have and what its context is to be. But, since this context is within time it can only be perceived on one occasion, not over and over again as is possible in the world of objects.

It is only because of the mental present that we are able to perceive the relationship of one sound in a melody to the sounds immediately before and after it, and we can only feel the shape of longer stretches of melody by exercising the powers to record and reproduce which the immediate memory possesses. Thus music, though it is not related to objects, is still concrete and tied to the senses but demands a mental agility which, since it is unrelated to objects, uses some abstract thought processes, yet steps over the boundary of pure thought because it depends on sense impressions. So it is not surprising that three to four year old children can only use in their imaginative play a small part of the scope which music offers them. The child is still scarcely capable of truly original creation. The reason for this is not only his comparatively weak intellectual strength, but also the attitude towards objective reality that is characteristic of a child of this age. So the fantasy world of music extends into the real world of the three to four year old child in the same way that he may invest actual objects in his environment with magical powers, as well as ask 'questions why' about them.

The two worlds meet in the many rhymes for dancing a child up and down on one's knees, in singing games such as 'Pat-a-cake', '*Heile, heile, Segen*' and '*Schneck im Haus*'.[1] Here a small corner of the child's world comes into contact with music in a way which fits perfectly with the imaginative world of two to four year olds. When they play round games, as children of this age go on doing for a surprisingly long time, they have the added pleasure of movement.

The extension of the world of music into the world of things is apparent in another way too. No less than 36 per cent of the subjects heard the pure rhythms in Test Series 3 as noises and associated them with things which produced similar impressions on the sense of hearing. The children also began to notice much more often the instruments which were used for the tests or which they heard on the radio.

We found from our observations in homes and in nursery schools that the wish to play singing games is so strong that no child asked to stop once he had started one of these. So, judging by the way the children enjoyed them, these activities must occupy an important place in children's experience. If it is true that these tendencies give an indication of what some of the objectives in helping the process of development should be,

---

1. A comparable English singing game to '*Schneck im Haus*' would be 'Snail, snail, Crawl out of your hole. Or else I'll beat you, Black as coal.' (Opie, *Oxford Dictionary of Nursery Rhymes.*)

'*Heile, heile, Segen*' is a German rhyme which an adult may sing to a child who has hurt himself. The nearest English equivalent would seem to be an adult saying to a child, 'Kiss it better'.

then singing and round games, as forms of music-making, should occupy an important place in the child's overall development, since they belong to that borderland where the worlds of fantasy and reality meet.

The importance of singing and round games in the development of musical talent, and their place in children's general development, has not yet been systematically investigated. However, it may safely be assumed that is is important to the musical, as well as the general, development of a child whether an obvious ability is cultivated or stunted. Since three to five year olds enjoy them so much, singing and round games must be a most appropriate form of music-making and of play for children of this age.

A valuable piece of empirical research might be undertaken into the serious cultivation of music in relation to imaginative play, in order to determine whether the educational result would in fact be the expected one if the two worlds of fantasy were deliberately developed simultaneously (H. Moog 1967).

6 · The Musical Experience of the Child of Four to Six Years

1. The General Development of the Child aged between Four and Six

There is no clear break about the age of four, as there was in the earlier years, and development goes on peacefully and calmly, in contrast with the upheavals between the ages of two and three (Busemann 1953). However, this 'peaceful' development does not imply 'standing still'. On the contrary, this is the age at which the child begins to learn about all aspects of his environment in the greatest variety of ways. Many new types of behaviour, the beginnings of which have been indicated in previous chapters, only come to fruition after the age of four; so much so that Charlotte Bühler (1928) considered that the third phase of early childhood does not begin until after the fourth birthday.[1]

The child of four or five takes in the world around him through the increased liveliness of his senses; his attention span is longer; he no longer stares or hears passively, but can concentrate if he wants to. This means that he can not only be more attentive to what he perceives, but he can also adapt his behaviour to a situation in a variety of ways, and that to a certain extent he is able to behave in a reasonable way.

Since his power of logical thought is growing steadily he is more and more able to recognize cause and effect and analogies; he begins to be aware of time and, although to begin with the words 'today' and 'tomorrow', 'now' and 'later' are used indiscriminately, the fact that these words are used at all shows how much progress he has made in this kind of thinking. By the time he is five he understands the meaning of the time on the

---

1. German authorities refer to the age of from about four to six as 'the age of serious play'.

clock in relation to his daily activities, and he may continue a game from one day to the next. Piaget (1948) calls the age of four to seven the age of 'intuitive thought' and he considers that one of the most important characteristics of thought at the age of four to five-and-a-half is the continuing need for thinking to be attached to an actual object or sense impression. As one would expect, considerable developments in musical experience are made possible by a growing awareness of time, and also by the development of thinking – which is gradually becoming less dependent on sense impressions, though still linked with them.

With the growth in the power of logical thought comes the ability to analyse the environment which the child perceives, so that he is more and more able to recognize things in this environment objectively. He has left his egocentric babyhood behind, and is increasingly able to subordinate himself to the demands of an objective environment. Until he is completely capable of doing this his imagination helps him to interpret the world around him. But his fantasy life still exists, side by side with this world of objective reality, and in contrast to it. Fantasy is still used to supplement the real world, or to give it a magical significance. This is the age at which children love fairy tales, and stories which mix up fact and fantasy. The child's concern for other people also comes in, in his love of fairy tales, as he re-lives the good and bad luck of the characters in the stories. So these stories give him a most welcome opportunity to live out his concern for and protectiveness towards other people. His need for social contact is also apparent in his speech, since he loves to tell stories as well as have them read or told to him.

Finally, these changes in social and emotional development leave their mark on music experience.

2. Movements to Music

Among the subjects aged four and a half we only observed 48 spontaneous movements in response to the tests, and these were made by only 22 subjects. With the children aged five and a half a total of 51 spontaneous movements were made by 24 subjects. Thus the number of subjects who made spontaneous movements in response to music remained more or less constant. Between the ages of three and five (24 of the three year old subjects made spontaneous movements) the number of subjects making spontaneous movements remains constant. But the number of individual spontaneous movements again falls off steeply, from 59 among the four year olds to 48 among the five year olds and 51 among the six year olds. The average number of spontaneous movements is about 1.0 (three year old 1.2, see Figure 6). The variety of movement declines from the middle of the fourth year of life (average 1.9 movements) to the middle of the sixth year.

In the fifth year the average variety of movement was still 1.8, in the sixth year it was down to 1.6.

The decline of spontaneous movements can only be clearly seen when the frequency with which the different forms of movements were made is taken into consideration. Children aged four and a half made the following kinds of movement:

1. Swinging one leg up and down   19 times
2. Tapping on the table   9 times
3. Swaying backwards and forwards   6 times
4. 'Conducting'   5 times
5. Clapping   4 times
6. Nodding the head   3 times
7. Hopping up and down   twice

With children aged between five and six the types of movement occurred as follows:

1. Clapping   33 times
2. Swinging one leg up and down   15 times
3. Hopping up and down   3 times

The following stages of development appear in the spontaneous movements of four to six year olds:

1. The motor responses to music which had, at an earlier age, been made with the whole body were only made eight times altogether by the five year olds (swaying backwards and forwards, hopping up and down). This kind of response only occurred twice with the six year olds. Movements of parts of the body are clearly the ones which occur most often at this age, but even these movements are very much weaker – and may even be so inconspicuous that they can only be observed by someone who is consciously on the look out for this type of movement.

2. Clapping, which had hardly occurred before the fifth year, appears to be by far the most frequent form of movement among the six year olds. This may quite possibly be due to a learned response. Clapping is often used in the singing games which small children enjoy playing so much, and as most of our five and six year old subjects came from kindergartens it is more than likely that they had learned clapping as a movement which goes with music, and so they clapped when they heard other music. At any rate, a large number of the children who responded to our tests by clapping would not have clapped of their own accord.

If the clapping of the six year olds is not taken into consideration only a very small number of spontaneous movements to music remain, and these few movements are weak and only made for short lengths of time. So the following conclusion must be drawn: by the end of the sixth year, apart from a few exceptions children no longer respond to music with repetitive spontaneous movements.

In order to find out more about the types of movements the children made – and how well these were co-ordinated with the music – than was possible from the few spontaneous movements which were observed, we played some of the tests twice to the four to six year olds and the children were encouraged to make some sort of response in movement, either by saying to them 'You are allowed to move around', or by the direct question 'Would you like to dance to it?' If this had no effect, we gave direct instructions like 'Go on, clap' or 'Go on, tap on the table' and showed them how to do it ourselves. Only a few children responded to the first invitation to move, and these hesitated to do so; those who did respond to the first command, to move around, were simply being obedient. They had been asked to walk, so they did. There was no natural connection between the music played and the spontaneous movements, such as we had observed in younger children. The children did not make any other movements than the dance movements which we had specially asked for; while, on the other hand, they frequently carried out our request to clap their hands or tap on the table, when we asked them to do this to see if they could keep in time with the music or not. Clapping and tapping were chosen for this purpose because they occurred most often spontaneously among four to six year olds, and because they are the movements which accompany many well-known singing games.

Of the four year olds 28 and of the five year olds 35 clapped to the tests, as we asked them to. There were four children in this group of four year olds who could not clap or tap in time with the music. The nursery songs from Test Series 1 were played several times to the children, who were either asked to clap or to imitate an adult's clapping. We think we can come to two conclusions as a result of the movements the children made, depending on the lead they were given:

1. The subjects clapped in response to the test music because they were asked to do so. The only motivation, or at least the most important one, for this activity was the request that they should do it – just as it was with the 'dancing'. Then they made any sort of clapping movements, sometimes not even rhythmically regular ones; so the movements cannot in any sense be considered under the heading 'music and movement' because, though they took place to music, they were in no sense instigated and determined *by* music.

2. However, some of the unco-ordinated movements to music which were made in response to our request did show some connection with what was heard. The children listened at first, or in between clapping to the music, and were clearly trying to clap or tap in time, but were unable to do so in spite of all their efforts.

Three of the four year old subjects did try to clap in time, as they were asked to do. Only one child showed no sign of trying to do this. Among the five year olds there were no children who could not keep in time, at least for a short stretch.

Of the four year olds 20 and of the five year olds 26 could either spontaneously, or on request, keep time with the music, at least for part of the time it was being played. Some were able to keep it up for only a few bars at a time, while others were able to accompany a whole song with rhythmically correct clapping, but clapped quite out of time to other songs. In these cases it was not possible to decide whether the child was not capable of keeping time, or was simply not bothering to try. Only four of the four year old subjects, and nine of the five year olds, were observed keeping in time throughout the whole series (B. Baldwin and L. J. Stecher 1925).

There is considerable progress, between the ages of four and six, in keeping movements in time with music. It is not only a question of all children becoming able to keep in time at least for a short stretch, but also a matter of the length of time the child can keep up his co-ordinated movements. A child who, at the time of his fourth birthday, can already keep in time with the music he hears for a short while learns to keep this up for longer between the ages of four and six. Finally the growth of this ability is shown by the fact that the number of subjects who kept time with all their movements, doubled between the ages of four and six (R. Liebold 1936).

Only one of the few movements of the whole body was made in time with the music. The movements of parts of the body were far more frequently in time. All movements made in time with the music were simple, repetitive ones. As long as it was a question of keeping with music heard, and not keeping time with their own singing, the children always kept the pulse and now and again a note of longer duration. Shorter note values were not observed, even if the song was well known.

Things were quite different when children were accompanying their own singing. In these cases they sometimes clapped the rhythm of the words. Exactly as with the younger children, the movements they made to their own singing were much better co-ordinated than those they made to music heard.

A few children were already able to alter the speed of their movements when the tempo of the music changed, but the individuals varied greatly in the length of time they were able to keep up the change. Occasionally children altered their movements according to the dynamic changes in the music, as well as to changes to tempo. About the same number of responses in time to the music occurred with all the series of tests except the noises.

3. Songs

The group of subjects aged four to five sang less than any other in response to the tests; we heard only 31 songs from the 50 subjects, and these were, with one exception, made only in response to songs which the children already knew.

The five year old subjects also, with one exception, responded by singing only to songs which they already knew. But the number of songs in response to the tests had more than doubled; this group of subjects sang 78 songs altogether.

There are two reasons for the sharp decline in the number of singing responses to the tests during the fifth year, and the sharp rise during the sixth year:

1. Since children only respond to songs which they already know, the number of their responses clearly depends on the size of their repertoire of songs.

2. The child is more and more conscious of whether he is singing correctly or not and tries to do so, especially if strangers are present. Since few families make a practice of singing nursery songs at home most children only reach this stage of being able to sing with confidence after they have spent some time at nursery school.

So the decline in the number of sung responses during the fifth year, and its rise during the sixth year, is only partly determined by the stage of development which the child has reached. In the very earliest years the development of the ability to sing does indeed depend on maturation, but from the age of three onwards success in singing depends more and more on the functioning of the vocal apparatus. The five or six year old can sing and can reproduce words, rhythm and pitch, at least recognizably. Ability varies considerably between one child and another and, as well as musical ability, the efficient functioning of the vocal apparatus undoubtedly plays a part. Moreover by the time he goes to the infant school every child can greatly increase his singing ability if he is given the necessary practice.

So it was no accident that we always heard the best songs from children who regularly sang at home with parents or with brothers and sisters.

Children sing of their own accord relatively well, if the same limited repertoire is sung to them frequently. Doing this does not mean cramming them in a way unsuitable for a small child, but fits in with the love of repetition which is characteristic of children of this age. A dozen musically minded parents agreed that small children go on asking to sing the same songs for weeks and months on end, just as they go on asking for the same stories over and over again. They want people who are close to them to go on telling them the same stories, even though they may have known these by heart for a long time.   When they look at picture books they look for the same pictures, and when they themselves draw they go on drawing the same things for a long time. Children go on playing the same games for several weeks or months. Some children with a much wider song repertoire – but who were unable to sing any songs really confidently – not only sang more inaccurately but less frequently. We had to wait patiently before we observed any spontaneous singing from these children.

Figure 13. *Imaginative songs for four and five year olds*

Variation of the melody of 'Lantern' (B— 5 years 7 months)

La – ter – ne, La – ter – ne, La – – ter – ne, ich
geh' mit mei – ner La – ter – ne
bim – mel a, bim – mel a, bim – mel a

Variation of the melody of 'Little John' (Ch— 4 years 6 months)

Häns – chen klein, ging al – lein in die wei – te
Welt hin – ein, Stock und Hut,
steht ihm gut, wohl – ge – mut.
Ach doch die Ma – ma weint so sehr,
hat ja kein Häns – chen mehr
be – sinnt sich das Kind läuft Haus ge – schwind.

Our research into the singing abilities of four and five year olds rests chiefly on tapes of songs which the children have learnt. It was made still harder to observe spontaneous singing because most of the tests were carried out in the school. A few children were recorded here singing away to themselves while they played, but by far the greatest number of spontaneous songs were recorded on visits to the subjects at home.

The spontaneous songs of these children were partly just trilling or humming away to themselves, as we had noticed with the three year olds, and these songs showed hardly any advance in their rhythmic pattern on those of a year younger. The 'pot-pourri' songs were also observed several times, but not as often as among the three to four year olds.

Imaginative songs, in which fragments of known songs are incorporated, occur for a great variety of reasons. It may be that a child only knows part of the song properly and makes up the part he does not know by using any words and an original melody; this happened often among the four year olds. With the older children, not knowing a song properly was much less often a reason for making up something new. These children made up words or tunes much more often than the younger children, to songs which they sang almost entirely correctly, either before or after their improvisation. For instance one boy sang 'The Birds' Wedding' with hardly any mistakes, and then went on to make up a coda, to 'La'. Children often altered the words of songs which they knew, for instance keeping to one sound from the words for a whole stretch of the tune, before picking up the right words again later. When they did this, the children hardly ever managed to get back smoothly into the song again; they usually stumbled over one to two notes and syllables before they picked up the proper song once more.

The children also altered the rhythm and the melody of songs which they knew, and sometimes these alterations went so far as to leave only the words of the original intact (see transcription of the song 'Lantern' in Figure 13). Rhythmic transformations like that in the second transcription in Figure 11 occurred more rarely.

Half of the children aged four and five were able to sing songs with several verses correct, or with only a few mistakes. (The 76 per cent of three year olds who were classed as being able to sing correctly referred to one line of the words only.) Most of the little mistakes made by these older children were cases of singing out of tune. A third of these small singers reproduced the songs correctly, but made the intervals more or

less too small. This fault was particularly in evidence in the singing of
K— aged four and a half, which is given in Figure 14, No. 1.

Figure 14. *Learnt songs of children aged four and five years*

1. Smaller intervals (K— 4 years 6 months)

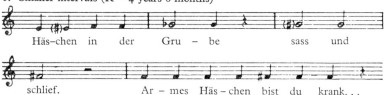

Häs–chen in der Gru – be   sass und

schlief.   Ar – mes Häs – chen bist du krank. . .

2. Out of tune (F— 4 years 7 months)

Ein Männ – lein steht im Wal – de ganz still und stumm. . .

3. Displacement of a line of melody in 'Hansel and Gretel'
   (U— 5 years 4 months)

Sie ka – men an ein Häus–chen von Pfef–fer–ku–chen fein

4. Return to original key after a wrong note
   (P— 5 years 7 months)

Auf uns – re Wie – se ge – het was,

wa – tet durch die Sümp – – fe.

5. Alteration of words of part of 'Hansel and Gretel'
   (C— 4 years 4 months)

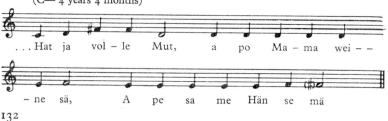

. . . Hat ja vol – le Mut, a po Ma – ma wei – –

– ne sä, A pe sa me Hän se mä

About 15 per cent of the four and five year old subjects had difficulty in singing a song they had learnt in tune. No. 2 in Figure 14 shows part of an example of this sort of out-of-tune singing. Displacement of a line of the tune also occurs often, as in the third example in Figure 14. After one out-of-tune note the whole of the next line of the tune is transposed Children of this age very rarely sing just one or two notes out of tune and then return to the right key (see Figure 14, No. 4). The few examples of this sort which we came across were all from children who were generally highly gifted. The ability to match the third- or fourth-from-last note of a line of melody, not the last note, demands an awareness of the passage of time which all children of this age clearly do not yet possess and which may help to develop intellectual abilities not connected with musical ability.

Mistakes in the rhythm were much less frequent than out-of-tune singing. About ten per cent of the children sang either very slowly or very quickly, but in either case the relationship between the different length of note remained correct. Otherwise mistakes in the rhythm always occurred in connection with out-of-tune singing. The children made even fewer mistakes in the words than they did in the rhythm, and these always involved saying a word which had a similar sound. Usually when a mistake of this kind was made the right meaning of the words was completely lost (see Figure 14, No. 5). So the overall line of development in singing (which begins with the words, adds the rhythm, and lastly begins to take notice of differences of pitch) is still apparent in the singing of children who are just about to go to school.[1]

4. Sound, Rhythm, Pitch and Harmony in the Musical Experience of Four and Five Year Olds

The attitude of the four and five year old to the world of sounds is clearly influenced by his attitude to reality. There is a marked tendency to relate what is heard to things and events in the environment.

The ability to recognize sounds develops greatly during this time. Of the four year olds 70 per cent could already associate the noises in Test Series 6 (Noises) with the thing which made the noise. Only 50 per cent of

1. Compulsory school attendance in Germany begins a year later than it does in England.

the three year olds could do this. Indeed, the sound was often associated with a thing like the one which produces that sound. Of the five year olds 90 per cent either got the noise right or associated it with something which made a very similar noise. Looked at negatively, however, this still means that 30 per cent of the four year olds and 10 per cent of the children who were about to go to school could still not identify things by the noise they made.

The tendency to identify an object by the noise it makes appeared also in the responses to Test Series 3 (Pure Rhythms).

About half the four year olds who reacted at all to this test felt that the clapping and the drumming of the rhythms was noise. Several children described it as horses hooves, while others thought people were quarrelling or that there were workmen making a noise. Among the five year olds the percentage of children who experienced the pure rhythms as noise dropped to a third. At the same time the number of children who responded to these tests musically – by making repetitive rhythmic movements – rose from 10 to 33 per cent.

When a child recognizes an instrument by its sound he is using the ability to recognize objects by the noise they make.

The ability to identify a thing by the sound it makes is also used when a child recognizes a musical instrument by its sound. The ability to do this is clearly as widespread as the ability to recognize noises made by other things, since all the children who had any knowledge whatsoever of several instruments and their sounds were always able to attach the right sound to the right instrument.

Recognizing a musical sound seems with many four and five year old children to be mental process of tying things together. When it happens, the situation in which the music was heard before is reproduced in the memory. Thus many subjects thought about going to bed when they heard 'Sleep, baby, sleep' or, when the pop song was played, they remembered that they had heard it before on the radio.

The attitude of the child towards reality was also apparent in the reactions in Test Series 2 (Combinations of Words and Rhythm). The words of the first two tests were concerned with Christmas and with birthdays, two events with which the child is familiar. Four and five year olds take a lot of notice of the meaning of the words; they repeat some of these, or explain in their own words what they are about, or ask what the test means. So children who are beginning to be capable of verbal reasoning experience these tests almost entirely as speech and only in a few cases as music. Speech helps them to understand the real world in which they live.

The imaginative singing of these children gives the impression that words, rhythm and pitch are beginning to be independent entities within the song, and that the singers are now able to separate each of these from the song as a whole and to handle them independently. Unless the different elements had achieved some degree of independence the imaginative alterations which these children make, when they make up new versions of songs they know, could not be explained. Two further results of the tests showed, however, that this is only a most tentative beginning of the ability to feel that the sound of the words, and that of the music, are separate entities. All the four and five year old subjects thought that the third test in Series 2, in which nonsense syllables were spoken rhythmically without using definite pitch, was music, and they reacted musically to it. However, five of these children showed uncertainty when they said that the tape was of children singing and talking.

So, for four and five year olds too, fixed pitch is not absolutely necessary for sounds to be felt as music when they hear the rich sound of rhythmically arranged words, though there are the first vague indications that the end of this stage of development is approaching.

When it was simply played on an instrument only 40 per cent of the four year old subjects recognized a song they knew. With the remaining 60 per cent, if the sound of the words was replaced by the sound of an instrument, they could not recognize the tune by its rhythm and melody. Of the five year olds 75 per cent could do this, but this means that a quarter of the children who were about to go to school could not.

So the dominant role which the sound impression plays in musical experience is maintained. Very often simply putting the words into a rhythmic pattern is enough to distract attention from their sense, and to make the children experience the test as music. Strangely enough, in their spontaneous singing the children will stick to a few simple rhythmic formulae which remain their models of rhythm for some time to come. The music which children of this age most enjoy listening to is also that which presents a rich sound with a plain rhythm maintained throughout the piece. The rhythmic models which the children like are almost all in duple time. They hardly ever use triple time in their spontaneous singing; but it is more acceptable in music which the children listen to, provided the circumstances are favourable. Additional tests confirm this, and showed that children always respond well to rhythmic training, and that they are able to copy much harder rhythms than their own singing would lead one to think they can. However, the well-known nursery songs do not provide much stimulus for children to do this.

As far as learning harmony is concerned, the tests gave an absolutely unequivocal result:

Children of pre-school age cannot yet experience any sort of harmony at all. They hear sounds, feel rhythmic patterns; and can also perceive differences of pitch, though not so clearly. The child is deaf to harmony at least up till the end of his sixth year, and probably for a long time after that. Not a single child showed the least sign of displeasure at the cacophonies in Test Series 5. They simply experienced this test as a sort of general sound. So the pre-school child still lacks the ability to analyse notes of different pitch when he hears them simultaneously, and to relate the individual sounds to one another, and our tests confirmed the similar investigations of Rupp (1915), Belaiew-Exemplarski (1926), and Stern (1952).

Bibliography

Abel-Struth, Sigrid,	Musikalische Grundausbildung, Frankfurt/Main 1967
Adorno, Theodor W.,	Philosophie der neuen Musik, Frankfurt/Main, 1958
Albersheim, Gerhard,	Zur Psychologie der Ton- und Klangeigenschaften, Strassburg 1939
Allport, Gordon W.,	Werden der Persönlichkeit, Bern - Stuttgart 1958
Anschütz, Georg,	Psychologie, Hamburg 1953
Baldwin, Bird J., and Stecher, Lorle, J.,	The Psychology of the Preschool Child, New York - London 1925
Belaiew-Exemplarski, Sofie,	Das musikalische Empfinden im Vorschulalter, in: Ztschr. f. ang. Psychologie, Bd. 27, Leipzig 1926
Bergius, Rudolf,	Entwicklung als Stufenfolge, in: Handbuch der Psychologie, Bd. 3, Göttingen 1959
Blessinger, Karl,	Musikalische Beobachtungen am Kleinkind, in: Halbmonatsschrift für Schulmusikpflege, 24, 1929
Brehmer, Fritz,	Melodienauffassung und melodische Begabung des Kindes, in: Ztschr. f. ang. Psych., Beiheft 36, Leipzig 1925
Brentano, Franz,	Zur Lehre von Raum und Zeit, in: Kant-Studien, 25, 1920
Bruhn, Paul,	Über die Frhüformen der Musik, in: Musische Erziehung, Kunstpädagogischer Kongress Fulda 1950, Stuttgart 1950
Bühler, Charlotte,	Kindheit und Jugend, Leipzig 1928, ³1931
Bühler, Karl,	Die geistige Entwicklung des Kindes, Jena ⁶1930
Bühler, Karl,	Tatsachen und Probleme zu einer Psychologie der Denkvorgänge, Teil I, in: Archiv für die gesamte Psychologie, Bd. 9, 1907
Busemann, Adolf,	Krisenjahre im Ablauf der menschlichen Jugend, Ratingen 1953
Cherbuliez, A. E.,	Die Musik im Leben des Kindes, in: Die Musik im Leben des Menschen, Basel 1941
Descartes, René,	Compendium musicae, Utrecht 1650
Dührssen, Annemarie,	Psychogene Erkrankungen bei Kindern und Jugendlichen, Göttingen, ²1955
Feuchtwanger, Erich,	Amusie, Berlin 1930
Georgiades, Thrasibylos,	Musik und Sprache, Berlin - Göttingen - Heidelberg 1954

Bibliography

Götsch, Georg,	Musische Bildung, Wolfenbüttel 1953
Grimm, J. u. W.,	Deutsches Wörterbuch, Bd. 6, Leipzig 1885
Haase, Otto,	Musisches Leben, Hannover - Darmstadt ²1951
Haecker, V., and Ziehen, Th.,	Zur Vererbung Entwicklung der menschlichen Begabung, Leipzig 1922
Hansen, Wilhelm,	Die Entwicklung des kindlichen Weltbildes, München 1952
Hanslick, Eduard,	Vom Musikalisch-Schönen, Leipzig 1854
Hartmann, Nicolai,	Ästhetik, Berlin 1953
Hegel, Georg Wilhelm Friedrich,	Vorlesungen über Ästhetik, in: Sämtl. Werke, Jubiläumsausgabe, Bd. XIV, Stuttgart 1939
Herbart, Johann Friedrich,	Kurze Encyklopädie der Philosophie, Halle 1831
Hüschen, Heinrich,	Textkonkordanzen im Musikschrifttum des Mittelalters, Habil.-Schrift, masch.-schr. 1955
James, William,	What is an Emotion, London 1884
Jöde, Fritz,	Ringel, Rangel, Rose, Wolfenbüttel n. d.
Kemper, Josef,	Stimmpflege, Mainz 1951
Kestenberg, Leo,	Musikerziehung und Musikpflege, Leipzig 1921
Kierkegaard, Sören,	Entweder - oder, Übers, von Chr. Schrempf, hrsg. von F. Droop, Leipzig 1939
Klages, Ludwig,	Vom Wesen des Rhythmus, Kampen/Sylt 1934
Kluge, Freidrich,	Etymologisches Wörterbuch der deutschen Sprache, Berlin 1957
Koenig, Adolf,	Die Entwicklung des musikalischen Sinnes bei Kindern, in: Die Kinderfehler, Jg. 8, Langensalza 1903
Kroh, Oswald,	Entwicklungspsychologie des Grundschulkindes, Langensalza ¹⁹⁻²²1944
Krudewig, Maria,	Entwurf einer Elementarstrukturlehre des Bewusstseins, Köln 1947
Krudewig, Maria,	Die seelische Gegenwart, in: Kant-Studien, 53, 1961/62
Krudewig, Maria,	Die Lehre von der visuellen Wahrnehmung bei Erich Rudolf Jaensch und seinen Schülern, Meisenheim/ Glan 1953
Krudewig, Maria,	Vom Stand der Psychologie des Gefühls und von ihrem bleibenden Ertrag, Berlin 1942
Krueger, Felix,	Zur Philosophie und Psychologie der Ganzheit, Berlin - Göttingen - Heidelberg 1953
Kube, Gerhard,	Kind und Musik, München 1958

Kurth, Ernst,	Musikpsychologie, Bern ²1947
Lange, Carl,	Über Gemütsbewegungen, Leipzig 1887
Leibold, Rudolf,	Akustisch-motorischer Rhythmus in früher Kindheit, Diss, München 1936
Lersch, Philipp,	Der Aufbau der Person, München ⁸1962
Lindworsky, Johannes,	Orientierende Untersuchungen über höhere Gefühle, in: Archiv für die gesamte Psychologie, Bd. 61, 1928
Lipps, Th.,	Das Selbstbewusstsein, Empfindung und Gefühl, Wiesbadan 1901
Löwenfeld, B.,	Reaktionen der Säuglinge auf Klänge und Geräusche, in: Zeitschrift f. Psych. und Physiol. d. Sinnesorgane, 104, 1927
Marbe, Karl,	Experimentell-psychologische Untersuchungen über das Urteil, Eine Einleitung in die Logik, Leipzig 1901
Messerschmid, Felix,	Melodie und Sprache im alten Kirchenlied, in: Zeitschrift für Kirchenmusik, 11. Jahrgang, Dresden 1929/30
Metzger, Wolfgang,	Der Ort der Wahrnehmungslehre im Aufbau der Psychologie, in: Handbuch der Psychologie, Bd. 1, Allgemeine Psychologie, Göttingen 1966
Moog, Helmut,	Beginn und erste Entwicklung des Musikerlebens im Kindesalter, Diss. Köln 1963, Ratingen ²1967
Moog, Helmut,	Der Bildungsinhalt Musik und seine Bedeutung für die Heilpädagogik, in: Päd. Rundschau, Jahrgang 21, Ratingen 1967
Nestele, Albert,	Die musikalische Produktion im Kindesalter, in: Ztschr. f. ang. Psych., Beiheft 52, 1930
Neugebauer, Hanna,	Kind und Musik, in: Ztschr. f. päd. Psych., 30, Leipzig 1929
Nitsche, Paul,	Die Pflege der Kinderstimme, Mainz 1952
Osterrieth, P., Piaget, Jean, u. a.	Le Problème des stades en psychologie de l'enfant, Paris 1956
Pfänder, Alexander,	Einführung in die Psychologie, Leipzig 1904, ²1920
Piaget, Jean,	Psychologie der Intelligenz, Zürich 1948
Portmann, Adolf,	Zoologie und das neue Bild des Menschen, Hamburg ²1958
Preyer, Wilhelm,	Die Seele des Kindes, Leipzig ⁹1923
Probst, Werner,	Vom Zukunftsbezogensein im Musikerleben, Diss. Köln 1960
Remplein, Heinz,	Die seelische Entwicklung des Menschen im Kindes- und Jugendalter, München - Basel, ¹³1965

Bibliography

Révész, Géza,	Einführung in Musikpsychologie, Bern 1946
Rupp, Hans,	Über die Prüfung musikalischer Fähigkeiten, in: Zeitschrift f. ang. Psych., 9, 1915
Sachs, Kurt,	Vergleichende Musikwissenschaft, Leipzig 1930
Scheidler, Bernhard,	Musikerziehung in der Volksschule, München 1952
Schering, Arnold,	Das Symbol in der Musik, Leipzig 1941
Schuenemann, Georg,	Musikerziehung I, Leipzig 1930
Silverstolpe, G. W.,	Zur Frage der 'Urmelodie', in: Ztschr. f. ang. Psych., 27, 1926
Spitz, René, A.,	Die Entstehung der ersten Objektbeziehungen, Stuttgart ²1960
Stephani, Hermann,	Zur Psychologie des musikalischen Hörens, Regensburg 1956
Stern, William,	Psychologie der frühen Kindheit, Heidelberg ⁷1952
Stirnimann, E.,	Psychologie des neugeborenen Kindes, Zürich - Leipzig 1940
Stockert, F. von	Über Umbau und Abbau der Sprache bei Geistesstörungen, Berlin 1929
Volkelt, Hans,	Versuch über Fühlen und Wollen, München 1930
Volkelt, Hans,	Grundbegriffe der Ganzheitspsychologie, in: Ganzheitspsychologie, München 1962
Volkelt, Hans,	Wesen der Gefühle, München 1937
Walker, Erwin,	Das musikalische Erlebnis und seine Entwicklung, in: Untersuchungen zur Psychologie, Typologie und Pädagogik des ästhetischen Erlebens, 4, Göttingen 1927
Wellek, Albert,	Musikpsychologie und Musikästhetik, Frankfurt/ Main 1963
Wenz, Josef,	Die goldene Brücke, Kassel 1949
Werner, Heinz,	Die melodische Erfindung im frühen Kindesalter, in: Wiener Akademie-Bericht Phil.-Histor. Klasse, Bd. 182, Wien 1917
Wicke, R.,	Die Musik in der Entwicklung des vorschulpflichtigen Kindes, in: Ztschr. f. päd. Psych., 32, Leipzig 1939
Wilbert, Hermann Josef.,	Die Förderung des musikalischen Gestaltungsvermögens im Kinde, Beitr. z Schulmusik Nr. 19, Wolfenbüttel - Zürich 1967